# Prayers
## *for* TIMES *of* CRISIS

PRISCILLA DOREMUS

© 2012 Priscilla Joy Doremus. All rights reserved.

A Seven Bears Publishing production, 2019.

ISBN:

978-1734425925 (paperback)
978-1734425932 (hardback)
978-1-7344259-4-9 (epub)

All Scripture quotations, unless otherwise indicated, are taken from the Holy Bible, New International Version®, NIV®. Copyright ©1973, 1978, 1984, 2011 by Biblica, Inc.™ Used by permission of Zondervan. All rights reserved worldwide. www.zondervan.comThe "NIV" and "New International Version" are trademarks registered in the United States Patent and Trademark Office by Biblica, Inc.™

Unless otherwise indicated, all Scripture quotations are taken from the Holy Bible, New Living Translation, copyright © 1996, 2004, 2015 by Tyndale House Foundation. Used by permission of Tyndale House Publishers, Inc., Carol Stream, Illinois 60188. All rights reserved.

All Scripture quotations marked KJV taken from the King James Version, which is public domain.

# DEDICATION

*This book is dedicated to you, the reader. May God use these pages to communicate His love for you and meet you in your time of need.*

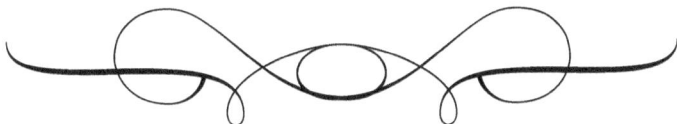

"So let us come boldly to the throne of our gracious God. There we will receive his mercy, and we will find grace to help us when we need it most."

—*Hebrews 4:16 (NLT)*

## Section VI: Prayers for Times of Physical Need ............ 113

A Prayer for God's Provision .............................................. 114
A Prayer for Motivation to Work ........................................ 116
A Prayer for Opportunity ................................................... 118
A Prayer for Shelter ............................................................ 120
A Prayer for Food ............................................................... 122
A Prayer for Employment .................................................. 124
A Prayer for Clothing ......................................................... 126
A Prayer Regarding Finances ............................................. 128
A Prayer for Favorable Weather ........................................ 130
A Prayer for Helping Hands ............................................... 132

## Section VII: Prayers for Times of Despair ............ 135

A Prayer for Hope .............................................................. 136
A Prayer when Tempted by Suicide ................................... 138
A Prayer for Love ............................................................... 140
A Prayer for Deliverance .................................................... 142
A Prayer for Laughter ........................................................ 144
A Prayer to Overcome Bitterness ....................................... 146
A Prayer when a Job Is Lost ............................................... 148
A Prayer when You've
Had a Great Fall ................................................................. 150
A Prayer when Facing Prison Time .................................... 152
A Prayer when Severely Depressed .................................... 154

## Section VIII: Prayers for Times of Loneliness ............ 157

A Prayer for Companionship ............................................. 158
A Prayer for Purpose .......................................................... 160
A Prayer for Effective Use of Time ..................................... 162
A Prayer in Time of Public Disgrace .................................. 164
A Prayer to Be Understood ................................................ 166
A Prayer for Someone to Listen ......................................... 168
A Prayer for Kindness ........................................................ 170
A Prayer for Times of Rejection ......................................... 172

A Prayer for a Godly Mate ................................................................. 174
A Prayer for True Friendship ............................................................. 176

## Section IX: Prayers for Times of Fear ........................................... 179

A Prayer for Protection ...................................................................... 180
A Prayer for Removal of Danger ....................................................... 182
A Prayer for a Hiding Place ............................................................... 184
A Prayer for Safe Passage ................................................................... 186
A Prayer for Defense .......................................................................... 188
A Prayer for Awareness of Danger .................................................... 190
A Prayer for a Sense of Reality .......................................................... 192
A Prayer for Protection by Angels .................................................... 194
A Prayer for the Protection of Others .............................................. 196
A Prayer for Removal of Jealousy ..................................................... 198

## Section X: Prayers for Times of Weakness ................................... 201

A Prayer for Strength ......................................................................... 202
A Prayer for Spiritual Growth ........................................................... 204
A Prayer for Dependence on Christ ................................................. 206
A Prayer in Time of Marital Crisis ................................................... 208
A Prayer of Repentance ..................................................................... 210
A Prodigal Prayer ............................................................................... 212
A Prayer for Humility ........................................................................ 214
A Prayer for Revival ........................................................................... 216
A Prayer for Families
Struggling with Addiction ................................................................. 218
A Prayer of Praise ............................................................................... 220

## Author Biography ........................................................................... 221

# Prologue

The overwhelming message of the *Holy Bible* is the picture painted by God of His massive love for all of us—every single one of us that He created. To that end, He has provided us with the opportunity to directly communicate with Him through prayer.

He gives us very specific instructions and examples on how we ought to pray in Matthew, Chapter Six, and many other places throughout the *Holy Bible*. The condition of our heart and the level of faith we have in Christ also have a direct impact on the effectiveness of our prayer life.

The *Holy Bible* says in Hebrews 11:6, "And it is impossible to please God without faith. Anyone who wants to come to him must believe that God exists and that he rewards those who sincerely seek him."

We must believe in order to be pleasing to God.

In my own life, I have struggled in this area. If I were a man, I'm sure my name would have been Thomas. I would have been the disciple who had to touch the nail scars of Jesus' hands. There have been many times when I have prayed this simple sentence prayer, "Lord, help my unbelief." Each time I have prayed that prayer, God has answered me by strengthening my faith. In each crisis I have faced, God has used it as a way of refining me into the person He wants me to be.

My father is a pastor, and when I was a little girl, I gave him a plaque which read, "Troubles are often the tools by which God fashions us for greater things." After many years of trouble from which God has always delivered, I know that to be true.

The prayers in this book are intended as a starting point for your prayers in times of crisis.

*"Those who plant in tears will harvest with shouts of joy."*

—*Psalm 126:5*

# Section I

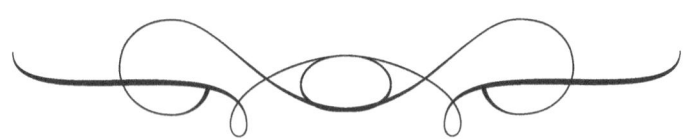

## Prayers
### *for* Times *of* Physical Illness

# A Prayer for Healing

In 2 Kings 20:1-7, the *Holy Bible* tells us the story of King Hezekiah.

King Hezekiah had become deathly ill, and the prophet Isaiah came to visit him. Isaiah had received a message from the Lord and was the bearer of bad news. The news was that King Hezekiah needed to put his affairs in order because he was not going to recover from his illness. He was going to die.

The *Holy Bible* says in 2 Kings 20:2-3, "When Hezekiah heard this, he turned his face to the wall and prayed to the Lord, 'Remember, O Lord, how I have always been faithful to you and have served you single-mindedly, always doing what pleases you.' Then he broke down and wept bitterly."

The story goes on to say that before the prophet Isaiah left the courtyard, the Lord spoke to him again. The Lord told Isaiah to go back and tell Hezekiah that He had heard his prayer and that He saw Hezekiah's tears. God told Isaiah to let King Hezekiah know that in three days he would be healed and would get out of bed.

On top of that, God promised to add fifteen years to King Hezekiah's life AND rescue him from the Assyrians! That's a pretty powerful demonstration of God's love. God has that love for you, too.

In the New Testament, everyone—every single person—who asked and believed for Jesus' healing power received it. Jesus healed them all. We may not always understand what true healing means for our circumstance, but we can know that God has our best interest in His divine plan. "And we know that all things work together for good to those who love God, to those who are the called according to His purpose." Romans 8:28 (NKJV)

*Dear Father in Heaven,*

*We praise your most holy name. You know the depth of the affliction we bring before you. We thank you for sending your son, Jesus, to heal all who asked and believed in the New Testament. Our prayer today is a request for healing, Father. We ask for your healing today for _____. We know that it is your will to heal_____. Release _____ from the grip of this illness and restore health to his/her body.*

*We ask that you help us, Dear Father, to understand the type and extent of the healing you desire to provide for _____. If you desire to provide ultimate healing, Lord, help us to be accepting of Your will. If it be Your will, give us a miraculous sign to reveal to us your plan and purpose in this situation.*

*Help us to depend upon You in times when we doubt, for you are the author and finisher of our faith. We thank you and praise you for the good you are bringing and will produce out of this difficult time.*

*In Jesus' name we pray.*
*AMEN.*

# A Prayer for Relief from Pain

The *Holy Bible* talks a great deal about pain. Jabez received his name as a result of his birth being so terribly painful to his mother. Job experienced extreme mental and physical pain. In Job 30:17, he says, "At night my bones are filled with pain, which gnaws at me relentlessly." David said in Psalm 38:17, "I am on the verge of collapse facing constant pain."

In Matthew 8, the *Holy Bible* tells of a Roman officer who came to Jesus seeking relief for his young servant, paralyzed and in terrible pain. Jesus told the man he would come and heal his servant, yet the man said he was unworthy for Jesus to come. The Roman officer said in Matthew 8:8, "Just say the word from where you are, and my servant will be healed." The *Holy Bible* goes on to say that Jesus was amazed by the Roman officer's faith. Matthew 8:13 says, "Then Jesus said to the Roman officer, 'Go back home. Because you believed, it has happened.' And the young servant was healed that same hour."

There are many different types of pain—physical and emotional. Each can be equally difficult to bear. We can be sure that God is with us during our pain, and He is with us always, "even to the end of the age." (Matthew 28:20)

Certainly, no one experienced more pain on this earth than Jesus. Yet, in spite of the pain he endured on our behalf, Revelation 21:4 tells us that one day, "He will wipe every tear from their eyes, and there will be no more death or sorrow or crying or pain. All these things are gone forever."

What a beautiful picture of the Savior's love for us.

*Dear Heavenly Father,*

*The pain is overwhelming! Help me, O Lord! Yet, we know that we do not bear our pain alone. For you, O Lord, bear our pain with us. Please grant relief! But, until that time, Lord, please help us to endure and see the blessing, the good and the refining that can come from this suffering and pain (Isaiah 48:10).*

*We praise you, Lord, in the midst of this pain and groaning because we know that in all our suffering you also suffer (Isaiah 63:9), and You alone can rescue us from this torment.*

*We ask for cleansing and forgiveness, Lord, that our prayer may be heard and received by You. We believe in Your infinite power, love, mercy and grace poured out in abundance for us.*

*In Your precious, holy name we pray.*
*AMEN.*

# A Prayer for Comfort

I love what the *Holy Bible* says about the Holy Spirit's loving, gentle comfort of His children. Psalm 94:19 says, "When doubts filled my mind, your comfort gave me renewed hope and cheer."

2 Corinthians 1:5 says, "For the more we suffer for Christ, the more God will shower us with his comfort through Christ."

We know the Holy Spirit is our comfort at all times, as the *Holy Bible* says in John 14:16, "And I will pray the Father, and he shall give you another Comforter, that he may abide with you for ever;"

That's right. It says forever. The Comforter will never leave us. If you need comfort today, claim that promise in Scripture, and receive the Holy Spirit's overwhelming comfort in your life.

Regardless our age, we all find ourselves in need of comfort at various times in our lives. I often envision myself as a child climbing into the lap of my Heavenly Father, to His warm and tender embrace, when I pray. His comfort is so overpowering and wonderful, especially in times of struggle and pain. Let Him embrace you as you pray through this time of crisis in your life.

*Dear Heavenly Father,*

*We ask for your comfort today and always. Give us a sense of your vision and the good You can and will bring to pass as a result of this difficult time. Comfort us with this truth, that You work all things together for the good of those who love You and are called according to Your purpose for them (Romans 8:28).*

*Lord, we know you hear the hopes and cries of the helpless and comfort them (Psalm 10:17). And, that even when we walk through the darkest valley, Your rod and Your staff protect and comfort us (Psalm 23:4).*

*We claim the promise You made to David in Psalm 71:21, that "You will restore me to even greater honor and comfort me once again."*

*Lord, we praise you for your mighty power and overwhelming love for us. May your comfort renew our commitment to serving You and others. May your comfort make us a blessing to others, and may we radiate peace throughout this and every circumstance we encounter in our lifetime.*

*We ask all these things in Your most precious holy name.*
*AMEN.*

# A Prayer for Acceptance Of God's Sovereignty

Sovereignty, by definition, is supreme authority. God has supreme authority over every area of your life. He has the power to act in accordance with His divine plan, regardless of our will.

Moses experienced this more than almost any other character in the *Holy Bible*. In the Book of Deuteronomy, the Third Chapter, Moses is experiencing the blessing of God's sovereignty as he completely defeats and destroys King Og of Bashan and King Sihon of Heshbon. The land Moses has taken in plunder from these two kings is divided among the Israelites who are to live on the East side of the Jordan River. God has now given His command for the Israelites to cross the Jordan River and take possession of the Promised Land.

Moses pleads with God to allow him entrance to the Promised Land in Deuteronomy 3:24-25, "O Sovereign Lord, you have only begun to show your greatness and the strength of your hand to me, your servant. Is there any god in heaven or on earth who can perform such great and mighty deeds as you do? Please let me cross the Jordan to see the wonderful land on the other side, the beautiful hill country and the Lebanon mountains."

Yet, God, in His sovereignty, denies this request from Moses. God allows Moses to go and look at all the land He is giving to the Israelites, but Moses is not allowed to enter. We may never truly understand all the reasons why God denies this request until we make Heaven our home, but we can know with certainty that God always has our best interest at the center of His plan and purpose.

*Dear Heavenly Father,*

*We praise you for your loving kindness, and we know You are sovereign in all things. Help us to understand and accept your divine plan and will for our lives and how this difficult time fits into Your perfect plan.*

*We thank you for the promise You give in Jeremiah 29:11, that You know the plans You have for us, that they are plans for good and not for disaster, to give us a future and a hope.*

*Lord, enable us to become who You want us to be, no matter what the cost. May we be willing to be poured out in order that You may fill us with more of You.*

*Help us to graciously receive your sovereign plan and will for our lives, Lord, and show us how we may act in accordance with that plan.*

*Forgive us where we have failed You, and keep us close, always abiding in Your favor.*

*We ask all these things in Your precious, holy name,*
*AMEN.*

# A Prayer for Wisdom in Treatment

Many times, when we are physically ill, uncertainty exists as to the best course of action. Often, doctors are unsure of just how to help us. In these times, we can find direction, hope and answers when we go to God in prayer.

Consider the story of Naaman in 2 Kings 5. Naaman was the victorious commander of the Aramean army. Naaman also suffered from leprosy.

No one in the land knew just how to treat or cure leprosy, yet a young servant girl knew a man of God, the prophet Elisha, who could help. Elisha instructed Naaman to go and wash in the Jordan River seven times. Elisha told Naaman that his skin would be restored and that he would be healed of his leprosy.

The plan of treatment from Elisha was not at all what Naaman expected. It was so far off base in Naaman's mind that he became enraged. Yet, when he finally yielded to the instruction from God, given through Elisha, the *Holy Bible* tells us, "And his skin became as healthy as the skin of a young child's, and he was healed!"

God can provide answers when we have none. James 5:14-15 says this, "Are any of you sick? You should call for the elders of the church to come and pray over you, anointing you with oil in the name of the Lord. Such a prayer offered in faith will heal the sick, and the Lord will make you well. And if you have committed any sins, you will be forgiven."

Like Naaman, we may not understand God's plan for our medical treatment, but we can pray and ask God to give us wisdom and understanding with regard to this treatment. James 1:5 tells us, "If you need wisdom, ask our generous God, and he will give it to you. He will not rebuke you for asking."

*Dear Father in Heaven,*

*We ask that You grant us wisdom regarding the treatment of this illness. May Your hand guide the mind, heart, and physical movements of any and all people who would impact the outcome of _____.*

*May we be open, O Lord, to a new and different direction for this treatment, if it is Your will.*

*Lord, we ask you to give us a clear sense of purpose and direction in this situation. We pray, as Paul prayed in Ephesians 1:18, that our hearts would be flooded with light so that we can understand the confident hope He has given to those He has called—His holy people who are His rich and glorious heritage.*

*We thank You and praise You for Your infinite love, mercy, grace, power and might.*

*We ask these things in Jesus name.*

*AMEN.*

# A Prayer for Development of a Cure

Throughout history, God has given people the power and authority to cure illness and disease. In the Old Testament, this power was often given through prophets and priests. In the New Testament, this power was seen often through Jesus and his twelve followers. Since *Holy Bible* times, God has given this authority and power to many whom some may consider unlikely.

God used Canadian surgeon, Frederick Banting, to pioneer the use of insulin for the treatment of diabetes. Frederick Banting had originally planned on going into the ministry, but God had a ministry of different sorts for Banting—medicine.

In the early 1920s, Frederick Banting had a new idea for finding both the cause and the treatment for what was then called "sugar disease." Through experimenting with dogs, Banting and his assistant, Charles Best, and others at the University of Toronto, were able to isolate insulin as both the cure and cause for the deadly effects of diabetes.

Although Frederick Banting and Charles Best did not eradicate diabetes, the diagnosis was no longer the death sentence it had once been.

We read about similar discoveries in the realm of medicine every single day. How merciful, loving, powerful and gracious is our God!

In Psalm 17:6 David said, "I am praying to you because I know you will answer, O God. Bend down and listen as I pray."

What an inspiring picture of the relationship David had with our Heavenly Father.

*Our Father in Heaven,*

*We come before you this day asking that you forgive us for our sins and reveal any unconfessed sins we may have in our lives. May we have a clear conscience before You today.*

*We thank You, Father, for bending down to hear us when we pray. Help us to listen to You.*

*Father, we ask today for a cure for _____. We know that you do not ignore the cries of those who suffer, as Your Word says in Psalm 9:12.*

*We thank You, O Lord, for empowering the men and women who have gone before us in developing cures. May you pour out Your power, authority and wisdom today on whom You please in developing a cure for _____.*

*Let Your grace, mercy, love and power be evident to all.*
*In Your perfect, holy name we pray.*
*AMEN.*

# A Prayer for Visitation

When a family member of mine was hospitalized in intensive care, another close member of the family indicated the need for visitation to cheer the spirits of the ailing family member. We were quick to load up the family and head off on the three-hour drive to the hospital.

The resulting visit was nothing short of amazing. We cried, we laughed, we talked of favorite memories, and everyone's spirits were lifted. This family member was also able to return home sooner than anticipated. I have no doubt that this was, in part, due to the wonderful visit, as Proverbs 17:22 says, "A merry heart does good, like medicine, but a broken spirit dries the bones."

It was the same for Joseph when he took his two sons, Ephraim and Manasseh, to visit his ailing father, Jacob, in Genesis Chapter 48. Jacob's health was failing rapidly, yet when he was told his son, Joseph, had come to visit, the *Holy Bible* says that Jacob "gathered his strength and sat up in his bed."

Jacob recounted to Joseph and his two sons the blessing that God had revealed to him in the land of Luz regarding the promise from God that his descendants would possess the land of Canaan.

Jacob went on to claim Ephraim and Manasseh as his own sons. He imparted a blessing to them, as well as giving an extra blessing to his son, Joseph.

What a glorious visit!

*Dear Heavenly Father,*

*We thank You for Your holiness. We ask that Your will would be done today throughout the earth as it is in Heaven.*

*May you grant a visitation of divine power today in order to accomplish Your excellent purposes. May you bring those You purpose in Your perfect plan to visit _____ today.*

*May the words spoken be words of refreshing, healing, and love throughout the visit, and may they accomplish Your will in the life of _____.*

*Lord, we ask that this visit and all others would be a blessing to all who hear and know of it.*

*May we draw and remain close to You forever.*

*We ask all these things in Your perfect, holy name.*

*AMEN.*

# A Prayer for Rest

Genesis 2:2 tells us, "On the seventh day God had finished his work of creation, so he rested from all his work." Doctors tell us that many of our infirmities are caused by a lack of rest. Even God rested.

The prophet Elijah needed rest. In I Kings 19, Elijah is running away from King Ahab and his evil wife, Jezebel, who has threatened to take his life. The *Holy Bible* says he went alone into the wilderness, traveling all day. He was tired and sat down under a broom tree to tell God how he felt. "I have had enough, LORD," he said. "Take my life, for I am no better than my ancestors who have already died." The *Holy Bible* goes on to say in the next verse that Elijah laid down and slept under a broom tree.

Elijah was so tired and hungry that he wasn't thinking clearly. After receiving the proper rest and food, Elijah was ready to go again. I'm sure he was glad that God did not immediately grant his request.

Often, we gain a more realistic perspective on our times of crisis with proper rest. If we are having difficulty finding the opportunity to get the rest we need, we can ask God for it.

In Psalm 55, David is overwhelmed by his troubles and cries out to God saying in Psalm 55:6, "Oh, that I had wings like a dove; then I would fly away and rest!" David knew that the proper rest would provide clarity to his circumstance.

The *Holy Bible* commands us to rest one day a week in the Fourth Commandment. If we can't seem to find the proper rest, we can claim God's promise in Psalm 127:2, "It is useless for you to work so hard from early morning until late at night, anxiously working for food to eat; for God gives rest to his loved ones."

*Dear Heavenly Father,*

*Please grant my plea for rest. My body, mind, and spirit are exhausted. We claim Your promise in Jeremiah 31:25, that You give rest to the weary. Lord, we ask that You provide both the opportunity and the ability for our bodies to rest.*

*We thank You for setting aside an entire day each week for us to rest. May we remember this day and keep it holy, as Your Word commands us in Exodus 20.*

*We thank You for the promise in Matthew 11:28, "Come to me, all of you who are weary and carry heavy burdens, and I will give you rest."*

*Lord, we ask that our rest be uninterrupted, and we thank You that we will be refreshed and strengthened for the tasks ahead as a result of this rest.*

*Forgive us for failing You, Father, and help us to forgive others who fail us.*

*We ask all these things in Your precious, holy name.*

*AMEN.*

# A Prayer for Good Care

The story of Hannah in the *Holy Bible* epitomizes God's good, loving and faithful care of His people. In I Samuel, the story unfolds, and we are introduced to Hannah, one of Elkanah's two wives. The *Holy Bible* tells us in the story that Peninnah, Elkanah's other wife, had children, but Hannah had none. Although her husband loved her dearly, Hannah longed to have children. To make matters worse, Peninnah would taunt her for not being able to bear children.

One day in the tabernacle she was crying and praying in deep anguish, to the point that Eli, the priest, thought she was drunk. Hannah vowed that if God would grant her request for a son, she would return him to the Lord's service for his entire lifetime. Once Hannah explained that she was not drunk, but in deep distress, Eli said, "Go in peace! May the God of Israel grant the request you have asked of him." And, God did grant her request.

Shortly thereafter, Hannah gave birth to her first son, Samuel. How overjoyed she must have been! Then, remembering her vow, I often wonder how difficult it must have been for Hannah to let go of her beautiful new baby boy.

God provided good care for Samuel in the Tabernacle. Eli, the priest, had two sons whom the *Holy Bible* calls "scoundrels who had no respect for the Lord or for their duties as priests." How unsettling the situation could have been for Hannah, knowing that she had given her firstborn son over to such an environment. Yet, as a result of Hannah's prayers, the *Holy Bible* tells us, "Samuel grew up in the presence of the Lord."

God can provide good care for us, too, wherever we are.

*Dear Father in Heaven,*

*We ask today for good care with regard to _____.*

*We thank You that Your Word tells us in I Peter 5:7 that we can give all of our worries and cares to You, for you care about us. We believe Your Word is true and ask You to provide good care for _____.*

*May you provide for every aspect of good care in this situation, just as You care for us and for Your church.*

*Lord, help us not to doubt, but to always act in accordance with Your will in all things. We thank You that Your Word tells us in I Corinthians 6:13 that You care for our bodies.*

*Where we are able to be Your hands and feet in providing good care for others, help us to be diligent in doing so.*

*We ask all these things in Your perfect, holy name.*

*AMEN.*

# A Prayer for Understanding

Often when we encounter instances of physical illness, we long for understanding. In I Kings 3:9 Solomon prayed, "Give me an understanding heart so that I can govern your people well and know the difference between right and wrong." And, the Scripture tells us that God granted Solomon's request.

In Psalm 119:104, David, Solomon's father, prayed, "Your commandments give me understanding; no wonder I hate every false way of life." David's understanding came from God's commandments.

We can ask for God's understanding in times of physical illness, as well. Proverbs 2:3-4 says, "Cry out for insight, and ask for understanding. Search for them as you would for silver; seek them like hidden treasures." If we lack understanding, the *Holy Bible* tells us that we can and should ask God for it, and trust that He will grant our request.

God wants us to have an understanding heart and to trust His divine plan. That doesn't mean that we will always know or be able to figure out why things are happening as they are, or how they will work out. Proverbs 3:5 tells us, "Trust in the Lord with all your heart; do not depend on your own understanding." God's ways are not our ways.

But an understanding heart will give us joy about the outcome of the situation we are dealing with (Proverbs 3:13).

*Dear Heavenly Father,*

*We cry out for understanding and insight this day. We trust Your commandments to be pure, holy and true. Father, please grant our request in order that we may have a clear picture of what You are doing in this situation.*

*We know that counsel and understanding are Yours (Job 12:13). We claim Your promise in Job 36:5, that You are mighty and do not despise anyone! You are mighty in both power and understanding!*

*We thank You that You expand our understanding (Psalm 119:32).*

*Father, we long for Your correction because by it we grow in understanding (Proverbs 15:32).*

*May the words of our mouths and the meditation of our heart be acceptable unto You, Father.*

*Thank You for the blessing of Your answer to our prayer.*

*In Your perfect, holy name we pray.*

*AMEN.*

# SECTION II

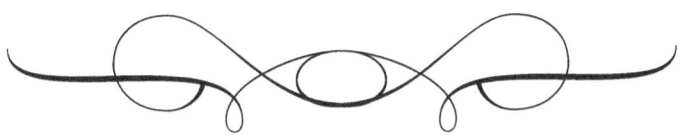

# Prayers
## *for* Times *of* Emotional Distress

# A Cry for Help

Emotional distress comes in many shapes and forms. Yet, regardless the form, it is painful and difficult to bear when we are in its midst.

In the Old Testament, David was no stranger to emotional distress, and cried unto the Lord for help repeatedly. Each time David cried unto the Lord, he was met by God's warm, loving embrace of him.

Listen to David's heart as recorded in Psalm 18:6, "But in my distress I cried out to the Lord; yes, I prayed to my God for help. He heard me from his sanctuary; my cry to him reached his ears."

In Psalm 31:22, David says, "In panic I cried out, 'I am cut off from the Lord!' But you heard my cry for mercy and answered my call for help."

In Esther 4:1, after Mordecai learned about the decree which Haman deceitfully dictated to have the Jews killed, the *Holy Bible* says, "When Mordecai learned about all that had been done, he tore his clothes, put on burlap and ashes, and went out into the city, crying with a loud and bitter wail."

Do you feel panicked today? Have your tears been your food day and night as they were David's (Psalm 42:3)? God answered David and Mordecai in their emotional distress. God stands ready to answer your cry for help, too.

*Father in Heaven,*

*Hear my cry and help me today, right now, Lord. My emotions overwhelm and consume me like a flood. Yet, I trust in You. I trust in Your strength, Your power, Your purpose and Your love for me.*

*I wait expectantly for You, Father.*

*Teach me Your good and perfect ways as a result of this distress, and draw me close to You, O Lord.*

*I thank You and praise You, Father, "For you are my hiding place; you protect me from trouble. You surround me with songs of victory" (Psalm 32:7).*

*Answer me in my distress, dear Father, as You promise in Your Word.*

*Forgive me for failing You, Lord, and restore to me the joy of my salvation.*

*In Your perfect, holy name I pray.*

*AMEN.*

# A Prayer for Solace

Webster's Dictionary defines solace as "comfort in disappointment or misery." From birth, our spirits long for comfort. The *Holy Bible* tells us in 2 Corinthians 1:3, "God is our merciful Father and the source of all comfort." The next verse goes on to tell us, "He comforts us in all our troubles so that we can comfort others. When they are troubled, we will be able to give them the same comfort God has given us."

We have all experienced or will experience a need for solace, for comfort in our lives. In God's divine providence, He has provided a Comforter, the Holy Spirit, who will never leave us or forsake us as long as we belong to Him.

The *Holy Bible* confirms this in John 14:16, which says, "And I will pray the Father, and he shall give you another Comforter, that he may abide with you for ever;"

What a wonderful demonstration of the Savior's love and care for us at all times and in all circumstances.

"Now may our Lord Jesus Christ himself and God our Father, who loved us and by his grace gave us eternal comfort and a wonderful hope, comfort you and strengthen you in every good thing you do and say (2 Thessalonians 2:16-17)."

*Dear Heavenly Father,*

*We thank You this day for Your promise of perpetual comfort. You are the source of all solace in our lives. We ask that You comfort us in our distress. We thank You that You will never leave us or forsake us, Father. How wonderful You are! We praise You for Your goodness.*

*Lord, may we climb into Your heavenly embrace and feel Your loving comfort surround us at this time and always.*

*Thank You for drawing us ever near to You. You are our hiding place, Father.*

*Forgive us for failing You and help us to remember that Your Word is a continual feast of solace for our souls.*

*Grant us solace, we pray.*

*We ask all these things in Your precious, holy name.*

*AMEN.*

# A Prayer for Self-Control

The *Holy Bible* says, "But the Holy Spirit produces this kind of fruit in our lives: love, joy, peace, patience, kindness, goodness, faithfulness, gentleness, and self-control" (Galatians 5:22-23a). Having self-control is one of the fruits of the Holy Spirit. It is something other people can readily see in our lives, indicating we have the Spirit of God living and breathing inside of us.

None of us are perfect when it comes to the area of self-control—especially in times of emotional distress. These are the times in which self-control is most needed; yet, often self-control is most lacking during these times. The God-given ability to maintain self-control is critical in times of crisis. The Holy Spirit can continue to refine us into the person He wants us to become if we will allow Him to control our behavior during these times.

Recently I experienced a time of emotional crisis and felt compelled to vent my hostility to a family member. The outcome was quite negative, and not at all what I expected. I realized later that my venting of the matter in this situation was sinful because of the intent of my heart. My intent was to expose the flaws of someone else, and this family member could do nothing to help fix my problem. What I should have done instead was pray. I was greatly convicted about my own lack of self-control.

Proverbs 16:32 tells us, "Better to be patient than powerful; better to have self-control than to conquer a city." Proverbs 5:22-23 says, "An evil man is held captive by his own sins; they are ropes that catch and hold him. He will die for lack of self-control; he will be lost because of his great foolishness."

Ouch!

*Dear Father in Heaven,*

*Forgive us for our lack of self-control. Help us to be held captive by Your great promises and truths rather than our own sins.*

*Grant us the ability to accept Your ways and transform our behavior radically into behavior that is pleasing to You and You alone. Fill us with the precepts and principles from Your Word, Father.*

*Lord, we are distressed and feel as though we are in a pressure cooker. Please give us an extra measure of understanding and control throughout this turmoil.*

*May You fill our lives until they are overflowing with You, so that we may exhibit and bear the fruit of self-control in our lives at all times.*

*In Your precious, holy name we pray.*
AMEN.

# A Prayer for Taming of the Tongue

I don't know about you, but sometimes I think I must have been born with foot-in-mouth disease. More often than I care to admit, my tongue has blasted at others like a bazooka firing at close range, inflicting widespread emotional distress. Then, conveniently failing to recall these times when others fire back.

The *Holy Bible* talks a great deal about our tongues and their power. James 3:7-9 says, "People can tame all kinds of animals, birds, reptiles, and fish, but no one can tame the tongue. It is restless and evil, full of deadly poison. Sometimes it praises our Lord and Father, and sometimes it curses those who have been made in the image of God."

The old saying, "Sticks and stones may break my bones, but words will never harm me," isn't true. Words can really hurt—like an atomic bomb or a missile at close range.

In the *Holy Bible*, David experienced many of these close-range missiles during his lifetime. During one of these times, he wrote, "My enemies cannot speak a truthful word. Their deepest desire is to destroy others. Their talk is foul, like the stench from an open grave. Their tongues are filled with flattery." (Psalm 5:9)

Proverbs 13:3 tells us, "Those who control their tongue will have a long life; opening your mouth can ruin everything."

How true! Have you ever felt as though the words you heard, either from your own mouth or that of someone else, seemed to ruin everything? I have. But we can take it to the Lord in prayer, and He promises to help us in our time of need.

*Dear Heavenly Father,*

*Please tame our tongues. Make them instruments of healing, encouragement and praise. Lord, we know that out of the abundance of the heart the mouth speaks (Matthew 15:18). May our words demonstrate a heart filled beyond capacity with love for You, Father.*

*Lord, we ask that You tame the tongues of all involved in this conflict. May peaceful words reign over all of us, Heavenly Father.*

*May the words we hear and the words we utter be a soothing balm to all, and may they aid in our discernment.*

*Lord, help us to know when to speak and when to keep silent that we may remain in the center of Your perfect will for our lives.*

*We thank You and praise You for who You are, Father.*

*In Your precious, holy name we pray.*

*AMEN.*

# A Prayer for Contentment

Many times, a lack of contentment can lead us into activities and pursuits which cause emotional distress in our lives. There is a story in 2 Kings 14 about a king with just such a problem.

King Amaziah of Judah suffered from a lack of contentment. He was a young man who had been successful in battle, having proudly conquered and defeated two neighboring kingdoms. He was on a roll.

Armed and freshly victorious, King Amaziah sent a message challenging his much larger neighbor, King Jehoash of Israel. Listen to King Jehoash reply to King Amaziah of Judah in 2 Kings 14:10, "You have indeed defeated Edom, and you are very proud of it. But be content with your victory and stay at home! Why stir up trouble that will only bring disaster on you and the people of Judah?"

Much like you and I, King Amaziah refused to listen to the warning of his wise neighbor, King Jehoash, bringing great destruction on Judah and the capture of King Amaziah.

King Amaziah forgot who gave him the victory. He didn't listen when God sent a messenger to warn him of impending disaster if he continued in his own strength. King Amaziah suffered from a lack of contentment.

Do you suffer from a lack of contentment? Sometimes God calls us to rest, trust and become content that He is working everything to bring about good in our lives—some way, somehow.

I Timothy 6:6 tells us, "Now godliness with contentment is great gain."

When we find ourselves in need of contentment, we can take it to the Lord in prayer.

*Dear Heavenly Father,*

*We are distressed and struggling with a lack of contentment. We know that is not Your desire for our lives. Help us to gain a heart that is completely content in every circumstance because our mind is stayed on You.*

*Show us Your will and Your way, Father. Help us to cease striving and know that You are God, as Your Word tells us in Psalm 46:10.*

*Still our hearts and quiet our distress, Father, as You teach us how to be content in You.*

*We thank You and praise You for Your mighty power in every moment in every day of our lives. Forgive us where we fail You and draw us ever close to You.*

*We ask all these things in Your perfect, holy name.*

*AMEN.*

# A Prayer for Release of the Situation

Recently, I had the privilege of learning about raccoons with my daughter. A particularly interesting fact about raccoons is their affinity for shiny objects.

One story told of a raccoon that spied a gold watch. When the owner discovered that the raccoon had taken the watch, he pursued the little robber and the spoil. Upon capturing the rascal, the owner found that the raccoon still held the gold watch tightly in its clutches. The raccoon was tranquilized, yet still held the watch in its grasp! Even upon injury, the raccoon held tightly to its prize.

Holding onto things is not necessarily wrong. It is what we hold onto that is often wrong. Are you holding onto a particularly stressful or distressing situation? Like the raccoon, have you refused to release your grip?

The *Holy Bible* says in Hebrews 4:14, "So then, since we have a great High Priest who has entered heaven, Jesus the Son of God, let us hold firmly to what we believe."

There is nothing wrong with holding on tightly, if the whom or what we are holding onto is our faith in Jesus Christ our Lord.

Do you have a raccoon hold on God? If so, releasing emotionally distressful situations will be no problem.

We can ask God to help us to release our grip on emotionally distressful situations and strengthen our grip on Him.

*Dear Father in Heaven,*

*Help us to let go of everything, circumstance and person in our lives and hold tightly to You. May we always and in everything cling totally and completely to You, Father.*

*Lord, we are distressed. Show us how to release the situation we face to You. We lay our burdens at Your feet, Father. We depend on the death of your Son (Jesus) to overcome sin and to escape hell. For we know that Your yoke is easy, and Your burden is light, dear Lord (Matthew 11:30).*

*Father, may we learn to release all things to Your infinite power and control, knowing that You will bring about Your perfect plan in our lives—even in the midst of trials. May we release our understanding and desire for a specific outcome to You, as well, Father.*

*We thank You and praise You for Your wisdom and peace. Fill us completely with You, dear Lord.*

*In Your precious, holy name we pray.*
*AMEN.*

# A Prayer for Stability

In times of emotional distress, stability is in high demand and short supply. We are often unable to see things clearly—as God sees them. James 1:8 says, "A double minded man is unstable in all his ways."

God doesn't want us to be unstable. He doesn't want us to be double minded in our thinking. He wants us to simply and completely trust Him. He wants us to get to the point in our relationship with Him that even though the entire world seems to crumble around our feet, we can rest in complete peace, knowing that He is in control of the instability around us.

We can't possibly know or understand all that God is doing for good in and through our circumstances. It all just seems so imperfect and crazy to us sometimes.

I Corinthians 13:12 says, "Now we see things imperfectly as in a cloudy mirror, but then we will see everything with perfect clarity. All that I know now is partial and incomplete, but then I will know everything completely, just as God now knows me completely."

God is the all-powerful stabilizer throughout lives circumstances and every crisis we face. We can pray and ask Him to grant us the ability to completely trust in Him as the stability in our lives. James 1:17 tells us, "Whatever is good and perfect comes down to us from God our Father, who created all the lights in the heavens. He never changes or casts a shifting shadow."

He never changes.

*Dear Heavenly Father,*

*We thank You for not changing. We thank You for giving us the power to know You and rest in You as our source of strength, peace, and stability.*

*We ask, Father, that You would grant us the ability to trust completely in who You are. Regardless of the cost, fill us completely and totally with You. May we hold nothing in reserve.*

*Help us to find peace and serenity in the chaos, change and turmoil around us. Lord, if we have contributed to or caused this turmoil in any way, we ask You to forgive us. Help us to make it right.*

*We forgive those who have hurt us and ask that they be able to forgive us for any and all perceived wrongs.*

*Dear Father, we thank You and praise You for loving us more than we can comprehend.*

*We pray all these things in Your precious holy name.*
*AMEN.*

# A Prayer Requesting Joy

"Always be full of joy in the Lord. I say it again—rejoice" (Philippians 4:4)! This verse doesn't say, "Be full of joy when you feel like it." It doesn't say, "Be full of joy when things are going your way." Being joyful is the fruit of one who is obedient to God—no matter what difficulties may come.

Listen to the heart of Job in Job 5:17, "But consider the joy of those corrected by God! Do not despise the discipline of the Almighty when you sin."

Let those words soak in for a while. Read the Book of Job. Job certainly knew an abundance of emotional distress. Yet, he also knew the character of his loving, Heavenly Father. Job had a deep, personal relationship with Him.

You may well be able to relate to Job. Think about the words in that verse again. God, as any good father, loves us so much that He corrects us. He lovingly guides us in the way that we should go.

David prayed in Psalm 51:12, "Restore to me the joy of your salvation, and make me willing to obey you." David understood what real joy was all about. He was a man after God's own heart. You can experience real joy, too.

*Our Father in Heaven,*

*We take joy in You. We take joy in Your correction! (Job 5:17)*

*We thank You for loving us enough to turn us toward You. When we ponder our many blessings, we are overwhelmed with gratitude and joy, Father.*

*We shout joyfully to You, the rock of our salvation (Psalm 95:1)!*

*May we come with joy and drink deeply from Your fountain of salvation (Isaiah 12:3)!*

*Lord, we thank You that Your Word promises that if we search for You we will be filled with joy and gladness. Hallelujah, Father, we praise You!*

*For we know, Father, that this light affliction, which is but for a moment, is working for us a far more exceeding and eternal weight of glory (2 Corinthians 4:17).*

*We ask that You restore to us the joy of Your salvation (Psalm 51:12).*

*In Your precious, holy name we pray.*

*AMEN.*

# A Prayer for Freedom From Oppression

It is so awesome and amazing to know that God sees everything. I was often told as a child, and tell my own children, that even when no one else is watching—God sees. He sees everything we do. He sees everything that is done to us. He knows everything that was ever done to us in the past. And, He loves us more than anyone ever has or ever will. Amazing.

When Moses was tending his father-in-law, Jethro's herd one day, he led the flock deep into the wilderness to the Mountain of God, Sinai. There, the angel of the Lord appeared to Moses in the form of a blaze from the midst of the bush.

Exodus 3:7-10 says this, "Then the Lord told him, "I have certainly seen the oppression of my people in Egypt. I have heard their cries of distress because of their harsh slave drivers. Yes, I am aware of their suffering. So I have come down to rescue them from the power of the Egyptians and lead them out of Egypt into their own fertile and spacious land. It is a land flowing with milk and honey—the land where the Canaanites, Hittites, Amorites, Perizzites, Hivites, and Jebusites now live. Look! The cry of the people of Israel has reached me, and I have seen how harshly the Egyptians abuse them. Now go, for I am sending you to Pharaoh. You must lead my people Israel out of Egypt."

Are you oppressed? God sees. Are you being treated harshly? God knows. We can cry out to our God and Father, Yahweh, who longs to deliver us into our own Promised Land. He hears.

The *Holy Bible* says in multiple passages that God is slow to get angry and filled with unfailing love and faithfulness. I have always found these words to be true.

*Dear Father in Heaven,*

*We thank and praise You for your unfailing love and faithfulness. We thank you that You see and know everything that is going on in our lives.*

*We ask, Father, that by Your mighty hand, You would reach down and rescue us, freeing us from this oppression.*

*We thank You, Father, that Your hand is not shortened that it cannot save, nor Your ear heavy that it cannot hear (Isaiah 59:1). Rescue us! Free us, Father! We are overwhelmed by oppression and harsh treatment.*

*You, and only You, can save us!*

*Forgive us for our sins, Lord, and help us to forgive others. Help us to forgive our oppressor(s). By Your grace, may we never be guilty of inflicting oppression on others.*

*We ask all these things in Your precious, holy name.*
*AMEN.*

# A Prayer for Salvation

There is no greater prayer in all the earth than the prayer of a repentant heart asking for the salvation that only God can give.

John 3:16 says, "For God loved the world so much that he gave his one and only Son, so that everyone who believes in him will not perish but have eternal life."

God makes it that simple. Repent, believe, receive.

And, if we truly grasp just a tiny bit of the love God has for us, we will want to spend the rest of our days in honor and service to Him.

*Dear Father in Heaven,*

*I confess to You that I am a sinner, and I am sorry for my sins. I ask that You please forgive me of my sins. I know that You alone can save me.*

*I believe that You sent Your one and only son, Jesus, to die on the cross for my sins.*

*Please come into my heart, Lord, and change me. I want to be new. Make me new, Heavenly Father.*

*I commit my heart and life to You. Teach me Your ways and help me to follow You all the days of my life. I make my heart Your dwelling place. Live in me and through me always.*

*Thank You for saving my soul to be in Heaven with You.*
*AMEN.*

# Section III

Prayers *for* Times *of* Death and Dying

# A Prayer of Mourning

There are few passages in Scripture depicting the great sense of love and loss as Jacob mourning for his beloved lost son, Joseph. Joseph, the family favorite, had been sold into slavery by his brothers, yet the brothers deceived their father into believing Joseph was dead.

Jacob believed that a wild animal had torn his beloved son to shreds. Genesis 37:34-35 says, "Then Jacob tore his clothes and dressed himself in burlap. He mourned deeply for his son for a long time. His family all tried to comfort him, but he refused to be comforted. "I will go to my grave mourning for my son," he would say, and then he would weep."

Do you feel like Jacob? God can help. He is the God of all comfort—even in times of mourning.

Dear Heavenly Father,

We hurt so very deeply! We miss _____!
We want him/her/them back here with us! The pain is too great for us to bear alone! Grant us Your strength to make it through this day.
Comfort us and keep us ever close to You.
May You work this tragedy into something good, some way, somehow.
Fill us with Your peace and Your presence so powerfully right now, Lord!
We need You. Surround us with Your loving embrace. We know that precious in Your sight is the death of Your saints (Psalm 116:15).
Fill us with an ever-present realization of Your divine plan and purpose—even through the midst of our pain. May we be able to find joy, knowing that _____'s life was not lived in vain, and the timing of their death was a part of Your perfect and divine plan.
In Your precious, holy name we pray.
AMEN.

# A Prayer for Renewed Purpose

The *Holy Bible* provides such a wonderful sense of comfort for us during times of death and dying when we are God's children.

2 Corinthians 4 reminds us to view things with an eternal perspective, and to renew our commitment and purpose to Christ with all the passion and zeal He gives.

It says in verses 16-18, "Therefore we do not lose heart. Even though our outward man is perishing, yet the inward man is being renewed day by day. For our light affliction, which is but for a moment, is working for us a far more exceeding and eternal weight of glory, while we do not look at the things which are seen, but at the things which are not seen. For the things which are seen are temporary, but the things which are not seen are eternal."

We can always have confidence in our eternal purpose when we have Christ in our hearts. God can and does continue His divine purpose for our lives, long after our death.

*Dear Heavenly Father,*

*Renew Your purpose in my heart and life today.*

*Thank You for the blessing of Your divine providence. Thank You for the assurance that You will accomplish Your will and purpose in and through our lives, even after our death!*

*Lord, please help us to commit to You at all times and not become complacent in our everyday living. Help us to do what we know we are to do in accordance with Your Word.*

*Grant us wisdom and understanding in knowing Your purpose for our lives and how we should act. Give us the faith to believe, even when we cannot see.*

*We praise You, Father, for who You are!*

*Draw us ever close to You.*

*In Your precious, holy name I pray.*

*AMEN.*

# A Prayer Thanking God For His Ultimate Healing Power

We all know that our bodies don't live forever on this earth. They wear out long before we would like for them to, much like a favorite pair of shoes or car.

My father, when confronted by such comments as, "You're looking old, Pastor," often responded with, "It's not the model—it's the mileage."

I've reflected on that comment many times, realizing that we all have different mileage limits. I've seen children that have endured more, in terms of their life's mileage, than I may ever reach.

I have sometimes struggled to understand what the *Holy Bible* tells us in James 5:13-15, "Is anyone among you suffering? Let him pray. Is anyone cheerful? Let him sing psalms. Is anyone among you sick? Let him call for the elders of the church, and let them pray over him, anointing him with oil in the name of the Lord. And the prayer of faith will save the sick, and the Lord will raise him up. And if he has committed sins, he will be forgiven."

Yet, now I realize that it is God's divine sovereignty that determines what *saving the sick* really means, and that we will all be raised up if we are His children.

There is such a thing as ultimate healing—completing our purpose on earth and heading heavenward to be with Christ.

Even amid death and dying, we can thank God for His ultimate healing in and around us.

*Dear Father in Heaven,*

*You are the author and finisher of our faith (Hebrews 12:2). You are the Creator of the unique purpose in which we can bring glory and honor to You.*

*We thank You for Your ultimate healing power. We thank You for continuing Your purpose for our lives beyond our time spent on earth.*

*You are the God who loves us in all Your plans. Help us to trust You and Your purpose at all times. Grant us understanding and comfort.*

*Again, we thank You for ultimate healing in our lives. May we always remain close to You.*

*These things we ask in Your precious, holy name.*
*AMEN.*

# A Prayer in Time of Unexpected Death

When I was a little girl, I had a friend named Renee Elliott. Renee had a beautiful singing voice, even though she was very young. She proudly and confidently sang her praises to God before the church congregation nearly every Sunday morning.

Suddenly, and without warning, Renee developed leukemia and died. She was only eight years old. Hers was a life so full of love, zeal, and promise. It was hard for anyone to understand why she was taken from us.

Yet, in all our misunderstanding and grief, God understands. He has a plan that has at its center our ultimate good—an ultimate blessing. We can be sure of that.

I don't have Renee with me here on earth, but she is still accomplishing God's purpose—long after her death. She still inspires me. She still motivates me. God is still using the life she lived.

Philippians 1:6 says, "And I am certain that God, who began the good work within you, will continue his work until it is finally finished on the day when Christ Jesus returns."

*Dear Heavenly Father,*

*Your name is most holy. We come before You, asking for comfort, peace, and understanding in this time of unexpected death.*

*Father, we do not understand why _____ was taken from us. Yet, we do know that You are working in and through our loss to bring about Your divine plan and purpose.*

*Comfort us in our grief and loss. Grant us wisdom and understanding. Grant us peace.*

*Help us to lean completely and totally upon You during this time and always, Father. Forgive us for our failures, Lord, and teach us Your ways.*

*We thank You and praise You for protecting us and providing for us in ways we do not understand during this crisis.*

*We ask all these things in Your precious, holy name.*
*AMEN.*

# A Prayer Upon Receiving a Terminal Diagnosis

Even in "worst case scenario" contemplation, it is difficult to grasp the complexity and wealth of emotion that accompanies a terminal diagnosis.

When my second child was six months old, I was diagnosed with a brain tumor and given approximately two years to live unless I received a high-risk surgical procedure. My family and I shed many tears over this and prayed many prayers. Now, over ten years later, I am convinced it was the prayers and God's grace that have gotten us through, and, by God's grace, I am still here.

Yet, others are taken from our midst. We know not why.

I often think of Susan G. Komen and wonder if she had any idea of the wonderful blessing that would become of her legacy. She has touched and blessed the lives of so many people through her own beautiful life. Still more have come to know her through her death experience.

We know not why one life is spared and another is taken, but we can have faith and trust in God, knowing that in His divine providence, He works all things together for our good.

David prayed, asking God to spare his life in Psalm 119:88, saying, "In your unfailing love, spare my life; then I can continue to obey your laws." God granted David's request.

If God chooses not to grant our request, we can take comfort and know that His plan for our life, though we may only have a glimpse of it, is far greater and more wonderful than we could ever imagine.

As I Corinthians 13:12 says, "Now we see things imperfectly as in a cloudy mirror, but then we will see everything with perfect clarity. All that I know now is partial and incomplete, but then I will know everything completely, just as God now knows me completely."

*Dear Father in Heaven,*

*We thank You for who You are. We thank You for Your immense love for each and every one of us. We thank You that one day we will see all things in perfect clarity, as You see.*

*Comfort our hearts and strengthen us as we face this overwhelming news. We ask that You heal us, and if it is Your plan to bring ultimate healing, please bring peace and acceptance of Your divine purpose and plan—too great and marvelous for us to fully comprehend.*

*May Your name be glorified and praised both now and forevermore.*

*We ask these things in Your precious, holy name.*

*AMEN.*

# A Prayer for a Family in Shock

When families encounter complete devastation through some catastrophic event, their minds and physical bodies can often experience a period of shock. It is at these times that we must intervene on their behalf in prayer.

Phinehas had the courage to intervene on behalf of the disobedient Israelites, and God stopped the ensuing plague, regarding Phinehas with righteousness since that day.

The *Holy Bible* also tells us in James 4:17, "Remember, it is sin to know what you ought to do and then not do it."

If we know that a family is experiencing a period of shock, we must intervene on their behalf through prayer, as well as any and all other needed acts of kindness.

Do you know a family devastated and experiencing shock? Intercede for them in prayer and in action today.

*Dear Heavenly Father,*

*You know the deep pain, remorse and shock being experienced by _____. We ask that You bestow Your comforting hand upon this family at this very moment.*

*May You place Your gentle hand of peace upon their lives in this time of crisis and tragedy and fill them to overflowing with Your love.*

*Father reveal to us the deeper needs of this family and enable us to meet those needs in abundance. May there be no shortage of Your provision.*

*Dear Father, carry this family to a place of blessing that is far beyond anything they could ever ask or think.*

*We thank You for hearing and delighting in our prayer.*

*In Your precious, holy name we pray.*

*AMEN.*

# A Prayer for Continuance

Have you ever felt so overwhelmed by the loss of someone close to you that you've thought, "I just don't know how I can continue?" Many people in the *Holy Bible* felt that way, too. Job is the one that quickly comes to my mind.

Job's entire family was killed suddenly. Everything he owned was taken away. He was disfigured. His wife told him to curse God and die! Imagine it. Perhaps you are facing that right now. You don't have to imagine it.

Listen to just the beginning of Job's prayer in Job 7:6-7, "My days fly faster than a weaver's shuttle. They end without hope. O God, remember that my life is but a breath, and I will never again feel happiness." That is how Job felt. Yet, God had a plan to bless Job.

Job was more blessed in the second half of his life than in the beginning! He had 7 more sons and 3 more daughters. The *Holy Bible* goes on to tell us that there were no more beautiful daughters in all the land. Job lived to see four generations of his children and his grandchildren.

God heard Job's prayer and his deep sense of anguish and loss. God gave him continuance in accordance with His divine plan and purpose.

God will give you continuance, too! He has a plan for you, too wonderful to be imagined.

"For I know the plans I have for you," says the Lord. "They are plans for good and not for disaster, to give you a future and a hope." Jeremiah 29:11

*Dear Heavenly Father,*

*I sometimes wonder how I can continue! I don't know how to go on!*

*Thank You, Father, that Your plans for me are good. Thank You for giving me hope. Thank You for giving me a future.*

*You are my source of continuance, Lord.*

*Help me to go on in faith, knowing You are my hope and strength at all times.*

*Thank You that Your mercies are new every morning (Lamentations 3:22-23)! I thank You and praise You that Your faithfulness reaches beyond the clouds (Psalm 36:5)!*

*I claim Your promise in 2 Corinthians 4:7-9, which says, "We now have this light shining in our hearts, but we ourselves are like fragile clay jars containing this great treasure. This makes it clear that our great power is from [You] God, not from ourselves. We are pressed on every side by troubles, but we are not crushed. We are perplexed, but not driven to despair. We are hunted down, but never abandoned by [You] God. We get knocked down, but we are not destroyed."*

*I thank You and praise You for the strength to continue within Your divine purpose.*

*In Your precious, holy name I pray.*
*AMEN.*

# A Prayer for Time of Burial

Growing up in the home of a pastor, I attended many funerals—both for those whose hearts longed to follow Christ and those whose hearts were far from Him. Some had lived long, full lives; and, some had been taken, seemingly in their prime. Yet, in each circumstance, the *Holy Bible*'s truths are matchless.

My father always used a combination of wonderful Scriptures when offering comfort at the graveside of those departed. The words from these passages offer immeasurable comfort to those whose departed loved ones have known a personal relationship with Christ. Yet, they prick, convict and spur those who do not know Christ into a deeper understanding of Him.

The passages of Scripture which deal with death are many. Here is a list of some of the passages of Scripture that both my dad and I have found useful:

I Corinthians 15:1-4, 19-26, 35-end of Chapter

2 Corinthians 5:1-10; especially verse 8

I Thessalonians 4:13-18

Revelation 7:9-end of Chapter

Revelation 20:11-21:5

James 4:8-10

May you find comfort in each word, and strength for the journey ahead.

"We are confident, I say, and willing rather to be absent from the body, and to be present with the Lord" (2 Corinthians 5:8).

*Our Father Who Art in Heaven,*

*Hallowed is Your name. We thank You and praise You for the life lived by _____.*

*We thank You that this life was not lived in vain, but that You have used this life to will and to work Your good purpose in the lives of those who remain, and also in the lives of those that are yet to come.*

*Strengthen us for the journey ahead, Father.*

*Comfort us, Father, in our deep grief and sorrow. Remind us of Your Word, Lord, that if You are our Savior, to be absent from the body is to be present with You.*

*Thank You for the promise of Your second coming, of a new heaven and a new earth, Father.*

*We thank You for the hope of the Resurrection as You remind us in I Thessalonians 4:17, that those who are alive and remain will be caught up together in the clouds to meet You in the air. Then we will be with You forever. Thank You for that promise, Lord.*

*Forgive us for our trespasses, as we forgive those who trespass against us.*

*We ask all these things in the precious, holy name of Jesus.*

*AMEN.*

# A Prayer for Patience with Others

When dealing with the death or impending death of a loved one, often we have become physically, mentally, and emotionally exhausted. To put it bluntly, our patience is shot—towards anyone and everyone, including ourselves.

Yet, the *Holy Bible* tells us in 2 Corinthians 6:6, "We prove ourselves by our purity, our understanding, our patience, our kindness, by the Holy Spirit within us, and by our sincere love."

Colossians tells us to clothe ourselves in patience (Colossians 3:12). James 1:4 says, "But let patience have its perfect work, that you may be perfect and complete, lacking nothing."

When we are lacking patience in these desperate times, we can ask God for it. He will give it to you. He wants you to be patient. He wants you to have joy! He wants to strengthen you in all areas of your life.

Paul prayed for the Colossians to have patience in Colossians 1:11-12, "We also pray that you will be strengthened with all his glorious power so you will have all the endurance and patience you need. May you be filled with joy, always thanking the Father. He has enabled you to share in the inheritance that belongs to his people, who live in the light."

2 Peter 3:15 tells us, "And remember, the Lord's patience gives people time to be saved. This is what our beloved brother Paul also wrote to you with the wisdom God gave him."

Our patience in time of extreme difficulty can be the tool God uses to lead the worst of sinners to salvation.

*Dear Heavenly Father,*

*Fill us with Your love and patience for others.*

*Thank You for being patient with us and leading us to salvation and repentance through Your love.*

*May you give us grace and rest through this difficulty that we may overflow with Your love to others.*

*We thank You that Your Word reminds us that patience can persuade a prince (Proverbs 25:15).*

*May Your divine patience, exhibited through us, bring others to faith in You. May You triumph in this tragedy, as You triumph over hell and the grave.*

*Make us strong and immovable, always working enthusiastically for You, for we know that nothing we do for You is ever useless (I Corinthians 15:58).*

*Help us to live in complete harmony with others, as is fitting for Your followers (Romans 15:5).*

*We ask all these things in Your precious, holy name.*
*AMEN.*

# A Prayer for Supporting the Bereaved

When a loved one is lost, there is often an irreplaceable hole left in the lives of those left behind. That hole can be physical, emotional, spiritual, and financial. The *Holy Bible* commands us to love our neighbors as ourselves (Matthew 19:19).

Jesus taught us to serve and give to those in need in the Parable of The Final Judgment, told about in Matthew 25:31-46. In this parable, Jesus tells how our service to others in need is also service to Him. This service is a show of Christ living in us and through us. It is a sign of His righteousness.

The Book of Ruth also speaks of our service and support of the bereaved. In the first chapter of the story, Naomi has lost her husband to death. Ten years later, her two grown sons die, leaving Naomi and her two daughters-in-law to grieve. Rather than leave her mother-in-law, Ruth decides to stay with Naomi and care for her.

As the story progresses, we meet Boaz, a distant relative, who decides to become the Ruth's kinsman redeemer. The kinsman redeemer in Old Testament days, was to redeem or buy back the obligations of the deceased family member. It was a very big responsibility. We don't find many kinsman redeemers in our day.

Yet, Jesus redeemed us by his shed blood on the cross, and He cares for us daily by meeting our every need. I love the beautiful picture of His care painted in Isaiah 40:11, "He will feed his flock like a shepherd. He will carry the lambs in his arms, holding them close to his heart. He will gently lead the mother sheep with their young."

We are to follow this example and care for the bereaved, just as Ruth cared for Naomi, and as Boaz cared for both. And, we can ask God to guide us through prayer.

*Dear Heavenly Father,*

*Help us to support _____ in his/her loss. Help us to show comfort in ways that are pleasing to You. Reveal to us _____'s unspoken needs that we may be better able to provide help and comfort.*

*Father, we ask that You carry _____ in Your arms, holding _____ close to Your heart.*

*May we be an example of Your love in all that we do to help. Help us to put feet to these words, Father.*

*Father open up the flood gates of heaven and pour out a special blessing in the life of _____, giving him/her physical, mental, emotional, spiritual, and financial strength for the journey ahead.*

*Grant us time to accomplish Your purposes.*

*Use us to be a blessing in his/her life. And, may _____ be a blessing to others.*

*We ask all these things in Your precious, holy name.*
*AMEN.*

# SECTION IV

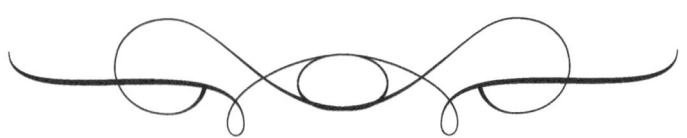

rayers
for TIMES of
CONFUSION

# A Prayer for Clarity

My daughter was getting ready for school one morning, when I noticed her glasses laying on the coffee table, smudged and smeared beyond belief. She quickly removed them from my grasp and placed them on her face.

"How can you possibly see anything out of those?" I asked, removing them again to clean.

"I can see just perfectly, Mom," she said.

Just perfectly. Ah, yes. How many times I have thought the very same thing?

"I can see just perfectly."

Have you ever looked into an antique mirror? The image is quite distorted versus what we see in a mirror today. Yet, imagine what God sees when He looks at you.

Do you ever say to Him in prayer, "Here are my requests. If You will please answer these, my life will be so much better!"

What you are really doing is saying, "I can see just perfectly, Lord," as you remove your smudged, filthy glasses from his precious hand of cleansing.

I Corinthians 13:12 says, "Now we see things imperfectly as in a cloudy mirror, but then we will see everything with perfect clarity. All that I know now is partial and incomplete, but then I will know everything completely, just as God now knows me completely."

We can and should ask God to clean our glasses. He can and will give us clarity in every area of our thought life if we will simply trust Him and allow Him to do it.

*Dear Father in Heaven,*

*Remove the confusion from our lives. We know it is not of You, as Your Word tells us that You are not the author of confusion, but of peace (I Corinthians 14:33).*

*Clean the smudges from our mind's eye, Father, and grant us clarity of thought. We thank You and praise You that one day we will see with perfect clarity, just as You see, Father.*

*Draw us ever closer to You, Father, for Your light gives perfect reflection into our lives. May we absorb and diffuse Your light into our lives and the lives of those around us.*

*Reveal to us our sin, Lord, and cleanse us from all unrighteousness.*

*Give us motivation and time to learn Your Word and gain the kind of real clarity into eternity that only comes from You.*

*We thank You and praise You for seeing clearly what a man does and examining every path he takes (Proverbs 5:21).*

*Grant our request, Father, in order that we may know and accomplish Your good purpose in our lives.*

*In Your perfect, holy name we pray.*
*AMEN.*

# A Prayer for God's Vision

Many times, in our lives we can experience a crisis of confusion due to a lack of God's vision in our lives, or a lack of understanding regarding that vision. Daniel was a man in the *Holy Bible* whom God had given the ability to see and interpret visions.

In the Second Chapter of Daniel, the *Holy Bible* tells us about King Nebuchadnezzar who had dreams that troubled him, causing him not to sleep. The king sought the counsel of his magicians, counselors, sorcerers and astrologers, asking them to tell him what he dreamed, and then to tell him what the dream meant.

The magicians, counselors, sorcerers and astrologers responded by telling the king that no one on earth could do what the king asked. This angered King Nebuchadnezzar, and he ordered the execution of all the wise men of Babylon. Daniel and his friends happened to fall into that category.

When Arioch, the commander of the king's guard came to Daniel, the *Holy Bible* says that Daniel spoke to him with wisdom and tact, saying, "Why did the king issue such a harsh decree" (Daniel 2:15)? Arioch explained the matter to Daniel, and Daniel went directly to the king, asking for more time.

Daniel and his friends pleaded to God for mercy that they might be spared from the king's wrath. That night, the mystery was revealed to Daniel in a vision. Daniel praised God for the vision, and the light that His wisdom brings!

God's vision is divine. It brings light into the darkness and casts out all confusion. We can pray, as Daniel did, for God's divine presence to bring His vision into our lives.

*Dear Father in Heaven,*

*We thank You and praise You for teaching us in and through the mysteries of life.*

*We ask that You bestow Your mercy on us, Lord, and reveal Your will in this period of crisis and confusion.*

*Come swiftly, Everlasting Father, and grant us Your vision to eliminate any and all confusion from our lives. Give us Your eyes to see. Give us Your vision, Heavenly Father.*

*Father, in Your mercy, may You also provide us the interpretation of Your most holy vision. Paint a picture in our mind's eye of Your plan and purpose for this situation, and for our lives, Father.*

*In all these requests, we ask humbly for Your mercy and grace, Father, that Your will may be accomplished.*

*For Yours is the kingdom and the glory forever, and it is in Your most holy name we pray.*

*AMEN.*

# A Prayer for God's Direction and Guidance

Yogi Berra is well known for saying, "If you come to a fork in the road, take it." We laugh, but often when we face that proverbial fork in the road, we are unsure of just which path we should take.

Psalm 32:8 tells us, "The Lord says, "I will guide you along the best pathway for your life. I will advise you and watch over you." Psalm 73:24 says, "You guide me with your counsel, leading me to a glorious destiny." And, Psalm 119:105 says, "Your word is a lamp to guide my feet and a light for my path."

Clearly in these passages and many others, God tells us that He is our guide, our map, our source for the right directions when we have lost our way or have questions.

When the Israelites were wandering in the wilderness, they were often confused and in need of direction, too, due to their lack of faith. But, in God's infinite love for them, the *Holy Bible* tells us, "The Lord went ahead of them. He guided them during the day with a pillar of cloud, and he provided light at night with a pillar of fire. This allowed them to travel by day or by night" (Exodus 13:21).

If we take the time to read our *Holy Bible* and spend time with God in prayer on a regular basis, we will find that God makes His direction clear to us, revealing it day by day. I love what the *Holy Bible* says in Psalm 16:7, "I will bless the Lord who guides me; even at night my heart instructs me."

Many prophets, kings, and ordinary people both inside and outside of Scripture have sought God's guidance and direction for their lives and have found it. Listen to what Azariah said to King Asa and the people of Judah regarding the Israelites in 2 Chronicles 15:4, "But whenever they were in trouble and turned to the Lord, the God of Israel, and sought him out, they found him." God will do that for you, too.

*Dear Heavenly Father,*

*We need Your guidance and direction in our lives. We are confused, and we know that confusion is not of You.*

*Show us the path for our lives, Lord.*

*Teach me how to live, O Lord. Lead me along the right path, for my enemies are waiting for me (Psalm 27:11).*

*Make plain to us the path of life both in this situation, and all others to come. Teach me to do your will, for you are my God. May your gracious Spirit lead me forward on a firm footing (Psalm 143:10).*

*We ask that You open the doors You desire us to pass through and close the doors that do not lead to Your perfect will in our lives. May we be accepting of Your will, Father, and help us to trust You with our lives at all times.*

*Strengthen our faith and help our unbelief. Guard us from the lies of the evil one.*

*We ask all these things in Your precious, holy name.*
*AMEN.*

# A Prayer for Wisdom

Solomon is well-known as one of the wisest men to have ever lived. People from all nations came to hear the wisdom of Solomon. But, why did Solomon receive this great wisdom?

In 2 Chronicles 1:10, Solomon prayed, "Give me the wisdom and knowledge to lead them properly, for who could possibly govern this great people of yours?"

God said to Solomon, "Because your greatest desire is to help your people, and you did not ask for wealth, riches, fame, or even the death of your enemies or a long life, but rather you asked for wisdom and knowledge to properly govern my people—I will certainly give you the wisdom and knowledge you requested. But I will also give you wealth, riches, and fame such as no other king has had before you or will ever have in the future!"

Solomon had a heart that longed to please God. God knows our hearts. He knows whether or not we desire to please Him. He longs to have a close, personal relationship with us.

In the midst of confusion, there is nothing we need more than wisdom and no one we need more than God. Take the time to draw close to Him. Take the time to stay close to Him.

Proverbs 9:10 says, "Fear of the Lord is the foundation of wisdom. Knowledge of the Holy One results in good judgment."

If we need and want wisdom, all we have to do is ask. James 1:5 says, "If you need wisdom, ask our generous God, and he will give it to you. He will not rebuke you for asking."

*Dear Father in Heaven,*

*I need your wisdom, desperately. I have lived without it far too long. Fill me with Your truths, Father, in order that I may know and understand You more.*

*Fill me with a reverence and fear of You and Your power that I may obtain a heart of wisdom that is pleasing to You.*

*Teach me Your ways, Father. Remove any and all confusion from my life. Make me like You—no matter what the cost.*

*Help me to keep my mind and heart set on eternal things, but may I not be so heavenly-minded that I am no earthly good. Pour out Your wisdom that I may know how to act in this time of crisis. Work out Your purposes in my life in accordance with Your wisdom and Your divine plan.*

*I ask all these things in Your precious, holy name.*
*AMEN.*

# A Prayer to Cast Out Satan And Demons

Satan and his power are real. I can tell you that from personal experience. I have seen him at work in the lives of people very close to me, attempting to thwart our efforts in obedience to Christ. I have seen him at work in my own life—tempting me away from the things I know are right, the things I know are pleasing to God.

Ephesians 6:12 says, "For we are not fighting against flesh-and-blood enemies, but against evil rulers and authorities of the unseen world, against mighty powers in this dark world, and against evil spirits in the heavenly places."

We must always be on guard against the attacks of the evil one. The best way to do this is through daily prayer, *Holy Bible* reading, and fellowship with other believers. Often people are drawn away from fellowship with other believers because of perceived hypocrisy. In such cases, because of sin, their consciences have been seared as with a hot iron (I Timothy 4:2). Their consciences are no good to them anymore. Their consciences tell them that evil is good and good is evil! We must, therefore, restore and admonish one another in love, strengthening our unity in Christian brotherhood—our unity against the dark forces of this world. I Peter 5:8 tells us, "Be self-controlled and alert. Your enemy the devil prowls around like a roaring lion looking for someone to devour."

Jesus cast out devils and demons on a regular basis during his ministry on Earth. He enabled His disciples to do the same. But there was an instance recorded in the New Testament in which a distraught father brought his son to the disciples for healing.

The father explained that his son had been possessed by a demon that caused him to have violent convulsions, grinding his teeth and foaming at the mouth. The disciples had been unable to cast out the demon. The father came and brought the boy to Jesus, who cast out the demon. Later, the disciples asked Jesus privately why they had been unable to cast out the demon. Mark 9:28-29 gives Jesus' response, "Afterward, when Jesus was alone in the house with his disciples, they asked him, 'Why couldn't we cast out that evil spirit?' Jesus replied, 'This kind can be cast out only by prayer."

We can follow Jesus' example and pray for devils, demons and all manner of Satan's evil influences to be cast out and removed from among or around us, and we should pray in this way as often as it is needed.

*Dear Father,*

*Please cast the devil out of _____, we beg of You. We thank You and praise Your holy name for You have not given us a spirit of fear, but of power, and of love, and of a sound mind (2 Timothy 1:7). We know that You are not the author of confusion, but of peace (1 Corinthians 14:33).*

*We claim Your promise, Father, that if we resist the devil, he will flee from us (James 4:7). We thank You for giving us the power to cast out demons in Your name. Father, we rebuke Satan's power; and, we rebuke the power of any and all evil influences over this household, this people, and this situation. Evil is not welcome here. It must be cast out into the pit of hell.*

*Guard our bodies, minds, hearts, souls, spirits and emotions from any and all evil influence and temptation. We thank You for making a way of escape for us in every temptation in order that we may stand firm in the way of right (1 Corinthians 10:13).*

*We bind Satan's power against us. We bind his power against this household in the name of Jesus.*

*We thank You for allowing this situation to strengthen our faith and our trust in You and Your divine power. Help us to be as shrewd as snakes and harmless as doves (Matthew 10:16).*

*We thank You and praise You for hearing and answering our prayer.*
*In Jesus precious name we pray.*
*AMEN.*

# A Prayer for Divine Revelation

Often in my life I have wondered why certain things were happening and just how they fit into God's plan for me and those around me. I was looking for divine revelation—an answer from above—telling me that what my mind thought God was telling me was, in fact, God speaking to me.

Gideon, in the 6th Chapter of Judges, was looking for the same thing. The Israelites had been disobedient and rebellious toward God for the umpteenth time. Because of this disobedience, God had delivered them into the hands of the Midianites for seven years. When they cried out to God for help, He reminded them through a prophet of all the times He had delivered them in the past—even after their rebellion. Then, God sent an angel to tell Gideon that He was going to deliver the Israelites from Midian.

Much like Moses, Gideon wondered if he had heard things right. After all, he was the runt of the litter as far as his family was concerned. So, Gideon asked for a sign to prove to him that God was going to help him deliver the people. When Gideon brought his offering, the angel of God burned up the entire thing. Gideon knew he had heard from God's angel. Gideon began to do the work God had asked him to do. He tore down the altar of Baal and the Asherah pole.

Yet, before Gideon went into battle against the armies of Midian and Amalek, he needed some additional reassurance. Judges 6:36-40 gives the account of what happened next, "Then Gideon said to God, 'If you are truly going to use me to rescue Israel as you promised, prove it to me in this way. I will put a wool fleece on the threshing floor tonight. If the fleece is wet with dew in the morning but the ground is dry, then I will know that you are going to help me rescue Israel as you promised.' And that is just what happened. When Gideon got up early the next morning, he squeezed the fleece and wrung out a whole bowlful of water. Then Gideon said to God, 'Please don't be angry with me, but let me make one more request. Let me use the fleece for one more test. This time let the fleece remain dry while the ground around it is wet with dew.' So that night God did as Gideon asked. The fleece was dry in the morning, but the ground was covered with dew."

God loves you every bit as much as He loved Gideon. We can humbly approach the throne of God's grace and ask for His divine revelation and guidance in our lives when we experience doubt or confusion.

*Dear Father in Heaven,*

*We humbly bow before You and come to You with thanksgiving, asking for Your divine revelation in our lives.*

*We confess our lack of faith, Father, and ask that You confirm, unmistakably, Your will for us in this situation. We commit our whole heart and life to pleasing and serving You, Father. Do not be angry with us, Lord, but hear our petition and grant our plea in order that we may serve You more and know Your will. Father may our actions be in accordance with Your plan.*

*Reveal Your perfect purpose in this situation, Father, for You know and understand our weakness. Help us to mobilize in Your strength, for apart from You we can do nothing (John 15:5).*

*As Gideon, we lay our fleece before You, Father, and ask _____ .*

*Thank You, Father, for your infinite unfailing love for us.*
*In Your precious, holy name we pray.*
*AMEN.*

# A Prayer for Godly Mentoring

We all need the loving, Christian guidance of other people in our lives, regardless of where we find ourselves in the journey of life. I have been blessed and changed immeasurably through godly people who have been placed throughout the path of my life.

The *Holy Bible* provides us with a beautiful picture of godly mentoring through the relationship between Paul and Timothy in the New Testament. Timothy was a young believer, well thought of by the believers in neighboring towns. He had been taught the faith of God by his mother and his grandmother. Paul, seeing the strong faith of the young man, saw his potential in serving God. Paul took Timothy under his wing as mentor, teacher, and father in the gospel.

Paul taught Timothy how to share his faith with all different types of people. Timothy learned what true service is all about, and he learned the deep joy that comes as a result of suffering for the faith. The two shared times of victory and blessing, as well as prison together, for the sake of preaching the good news.

Throughout their relationship, Paul encouraged, admonished, instructed, warned, listened, and guided Timothy along the journey that would enable each to fulfill Christ's purpose.

When there is no one around, and we find ourselves in a period of isolation, we can look to the Books of the Prophets in the Old Testament to mentor us along the path of life. And, we can look to God to provide us with a mentor, as He is the author and finisher of our faith.

*Dear Heavenly Father,*

*We thank You and praise You for being our mentor and instructor. We thank You that Your Word says, "even at night my heart instructs me" (Psalm 16:7). We know that instruction comes from You, Father.*

*Lord, we ask that You bring godly people into our path to help instruct us, guide us, and train us in accordance with Your Word. Bring a strong fellowship of believers to mentor us along our life's journey in order that we may fulfill Your purpose and plan for this life You have given.*

*Strengthen us, Father, for every good deed that You have planned. Prepare us and help us to prepare others for Your service.*

*Give us a true servant's attitude, Father, as You provided the example. May You pour out all selfishness in our lives and fill us to overflowing with You.*

*Show us who we should follow, Father, and teach us to make right judgments (Jeremiah 11:20). Remind us to test all things that are said to prove whether they are in accordance with Your Word (I Thessalonians 5:21).*

*We ask these things in Jesus precious name.*
*AMEN.*

# A Prayer for Epiphany

Epiphany, unlike a divine revelation, is an "Aha!" moment in your consciousness. But, like divine revelation, both are given by God. When we are facing times of confusion or lack understanding, we can ask God to give us an "Aha!" in our thinking.

In my own experience, many moments of epiphany have come to me when reading the *Holy Bible*. I have come to a passage of Scripture that I did not really understand fully, and after times of prayer and reflection they become so very clear, invoking an, "I get it, Lord! I get it now!"

Have you ever felt that way? Are you at one of those places in your life now where you are just uncertain about things? Do you find yourself in need of an "Aha!" moment?

I love Matthew 16 which illustrates Simon Peter's moment of epiphany regarding who Jesus really was. Jesus had been frustrated after talking with the Pharisees and Sadducees who had demanded that Jesus show some miraculous sign as proof of His identity. Jesus then asked the disciples, "Who do people say that the Son of Man is?" The disciples responded in Matthew 16:14 with, "Well," they replied, "some say John the Baptist, some say Elijah, and others say Jeremiah or one of the other prophets."

Then, Jesus asked the disciples, "But who do you say that I am?" Notice that Jesus asked all the disciples in his presence, yet only one of them responded. It was Simon Peter. Matthew 16:16 says, "Simon Peter answered, 'You are the Messiah, the Son of the living God.'"

Jesus' response is beautiful. Matthew 16:17-19 says, "Jesus replied, 'You are blessed, Simon son of John, because my Father in heaven has revealed this to you. You did not learn this from any human being. Now I say to you that you are Peter (which means 'rock'), and upon this rock I will build my church, and all the powers of hell will not conquer it. And I will give you the keys of the Kingdom of Heaven. Whatever you forbid on earth will be forbidden in heaven, and whatever you permit on earth will be permitted in heaven.'" Simon Peter got it!

*Dear Heavenly Father,*

*Please help me to "get it!" Whatever it takes, Lord, I pray that Your loving, gentle, kind, merciful, and skillful hand would guide me to an epiphany in this situation.*

*Help me to realize more of You, Lord. Make me more like You.*

*Give me an understanding of You, Father, and erase all confusion. Show me how to prepare for an epiphany in my life, Father.*

*I claim Your promise in Isaiah 40:5, that Your glory will be revealed and that all the people will see it together.*

*I thank You, Father, that flesh and blood do not reveal things to us, but that You make things known by Your Holy Spirit (Matthew 16:17). Forgive us where we fall short and draw us ever closer to You.*

*We ask all these things in Your precious, holy name.*
*AMEN.*

# A Prayer for Illumination of Our Path

The *Holy Bible* says in Psalm 119:105, "Thy word is a lamp unto my feet, and a light unto my path."

Once, our family went on a camping trip in a beautiful, heavily wooded state park. During the night, my seven-year-old woke me, as he needed a bathroom break. I felt around the bottom of the tent for the flashlight and pushed the button. Nothing happened. I was certain I checked to make sure it was working before we left. I tried again. Still, nothing happened.

"Come on, Sweet Pea," I said. "We're going to have to feel our way to the bath house." As we started along the dark path, we tripped over rocks and bumped into trees. How I kicked myself for not bringing an extra set of batteries!

In the distance, we could see a faint light that we hoped was the bath house, but we could see nothing along our pathway. Even the light of the moon and stars was obscured by the massive pine trees and thick underbrush.

By the time we finally made it to the bath house in the forest, we were scraped, scratched, stressed and thankful. If only I had been wise and prepared properly.

It is a simple example, but like the parable of the ten virgins in Matthew 25, it illustrates our foolishness at not keeping Christ as the constant illuminating source for our lives.

When the Israelites built the Tabernacle, they were commanded to bring pure oil of pressed olives to keep the lamps burning continually (Exodus 27:20). That lamp was both symbolic and practical.

If we spend time developing a personal relationship with God, He illuminates our path. Psalm 18:28 says, "You light a lamp for me. The Lord, my God, lights up my darkness."

Since Christ is the light of the world (John 8:12), He can illuminate your path, too.

*Dear Father in Heaven,*

*We thank You for being the light of world. We thank You and praise You for illuminating our path as You did that of Paul on the road to Damascus (Acts 9).*

*We ask that You make our hearts soft and pliable as we read Your word in order that it may be a light to our path. Help us to be obedient to the things that we read in Your word, too, Father. Thank You for showing us the great error of our ways and turning us from our sin through the power of Your holy word, Lord.*

*Father, we ask that You keep us firmly rooted and grounded in Your word daily that You may be able to illuminate our path daily.*

*We thank You and praise You for breaking the power of death and illuminating the way of life and immortality through Your Son (2 Timothy 1:10). May we forever walk in the light as You are in the light, that we may have fellowship with each other and be cleansed from sin (1 John 1:7).*

*We ask all these things in the name of the Father, the Son, and the Holy Spirit. AMEN.*

# A Prayer of Commitment

Since we know that confusion is not of God, then we can be sure that confusion has developed in our lives as a direct result of our lack of commitment to Christ. This does not mean that once we are completely committed to Christ, we will know everything and never have questions. What it does mean is we will know exactly who holds all the answers, and we will have complete faith and trust in Him.

God referred to His commitment to us in the *Holy Bible*. It was often called His covenant. A covenant is a promise whereby only the covenanter is bound to act. When God entered into covenant relationship with Noah after the flood, there was no requirement on Noah's part to act. God simply made a covenant that He would never again destroy the world by flood. There was no condition to God's promise. God even set His rainbow in the sky as a symbol of His covenant with Noah. Noah didn't have to act a certain way. He didn't have to live a sinless life after the flood. God didn't require anything of Noah; but, God knew that Noah had an obedient heart and was committed to follow God anywhere and do whatever He required.

Are you willing to follow God anywhere? Are you committed to following Him through any circumstance? Do you trust Him—even through the crisis you are facing?

When we are experiencing a time of crisis in our lives, we need to experience the strength, security, stability and comfort of Christ working in and through our life's circumstances. When we read His Word, we find that comfort. If we commit to Him in love and faith, believing that He will work all things together for our good, we will experience true joy—even in the midst of crisis.

*Dear Heavenly Father,*

*Today I commit my life—every part of it—totally and completely to You. I sacrifice my stubborn will and my selfish desires on the altar of Your grace, mercy, and love.*

*Father help me to be unwavering in my faith, trust and commitment to You. Keep me close to You at all times. Help me through this crisis. Help me to remain on Your path through any crisis I may face in the future, too, Father.*

*I commit to Your plan, Father. I give up my plans today, Father, and I choose Your plans for my life instead.*

*Father, today I choose to be totally committed to the mystery of the faith now revealed through Your Holy Spirit and live with a clear conscience (1 Timothy 3:9).*

*Help me to prove my commitment to You through service to You, as Jesus proved His commitment in doing good deeds (Titus 2:14).*

*We ask all these things in Your precious, holy name.*
*AMEN.*

# SECTION V

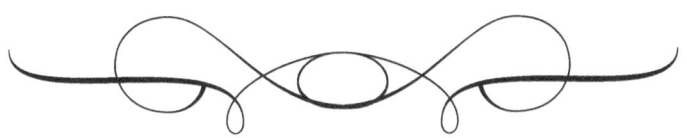

# Prayers
## for TIMES of CONFLICT

# A Prayer when Overwhelmed by Anger

Have you ever been so angry and enraged that you felt you would explode if you didn't act on your emotions? Many people in the *Holy Bible* did, too. In fact, the *Holy Bible* talks a great deal about anger. The words "anger" or "angry" are found 453 times in the New Living Translation of the *Holy Bible*.

Many times, there are very valid reasons for becoming angry. Jesus felt anger when he chased the moneychangers out of the Temple. There is nothing wrong with the emotion of anger, but we must control our actions as a result of the emotion. Ephesians 4:26-27 says, "And 'don't sin by letting anger control you.' Don't let the sun go down while you are still angry, for anger gives a foothold to the devil."

Cain had a problem with anger. He allowed it to control him. The *Holy Bible* tells us that one day Cain brought some of his crops as a gift to the Lord. His younger brother, Abel, also brought a present, but it was the best of his firstborn lambs. Genesis 4:5 tells us that God did not accept Cain or his gift. Cain became very angry and gave in to the temptation to sin. He murdered his brother.

Perhaps you have already committed a sin with great consequences just like Cain did. The good news is that God forgives. He sent His son, Jesus, to die for you and pay the eternal penalty for your sin. The bad news is that we must still face the earthly consequences for our actions.

If you are overwhelmed by anger now, but have not yet sinned, remember that, "The temptations in your life are no different from what others experience. And God is faithful. He will not allow the temptation to be more than you can stand. When you are tempted, he will show you a way out so that you can endure." (1 Corinthians 10:13)

*Dear Father in Heaven,*

*I am overwhelmed with anger. Please show me the way out. I do not want to sin. Help me to have self-control in this situation. Vindicate me and show me the path I should take in this situation.*

*Father protect me from evil desires. Forgive me for the desire to do wrong. Keep me on Your path of life.*

*Comfort my heart with the knowledge that You are in complete control of this situation, and that You can and do work all things together for good for those who love You and are called according to Your purpose (Romans 8:28). Thank You, Father, that I am called according to Your purpose. Thank You that You have a plan and a purpose for my life, and that You can bring good out of this situation.*

*You are awesome and all-powerful, Father, and I praise You for delivering me from the temptation to sin again as a result of my anger.*

*I give You control over my mind, body, will and emotions, Father. Fill me with the fruit of Your Spirit which is love, joy, peace, patience, kindness, goodness, faithfulness, gentleness, and self-control.*

*We ask all these things in Your precious, holy name.*
*AMEN.*

# A Prayer in Time of War

Ecclesiastes Chapter 3 tells us that there is a season for everything, a time for every activity given under heaven. There is "a time for war and a time for peace" (Ecclesiastes 3:8).

War is not something enjoyable, but because of the fall of man and our sinful nature, it is sometimes necessary in bringing about a desired outcome—a change. War is also not something to be entered into lightly. The *Holy Bible* says we are to prepare and to seek wise counsel before going to war. Proverbs 24:6 says, "So don't go to war without wise guidance; victory depends on having many advisers."

There are many instances in the *Holy Bible* in which God specifically used people who were not well-equipped, strong, or mighty in number, to win a war. This was done to show the mighty power and sovereignty of God. We must always remember that no matter how much we prepare for battle, the victory rests with God alone. He is our strength.

Perhaps you are a soldier at war right now, or you have a loved one at war. Maybe it is a spiritual war you are fighting. Perhaps you are overwhelmed with fear and uncertainty about the circumstance you are facing this very minute. God can help you.

2 Timothy 2:3 reminds us to, "Endure suffering along with me, as a good soldier of Christ Jesus." Things will not always be easy; however, we can find comfort knowing that the victory is ALWAYS the Lord's.

"My victory and honor come from God alone. He is my refuge, a rock where no enemy can reach me" (Psalm 62:7).

*Dear Heavenly Father,*

*We thank You for giving us victory through Your son, Jesus Christ. We praise You for overcoming the world (John 16:33).*

*We ask, Father, that You would provide us with wise counsel. Speak to our hearts, lead us, guide us, and direct us in accordance with Your perfect will. You know our fears, Father, and we ask that Your perfect love would cast out all fear (1 John 4:18).*

*Lord, we ask that this time of war would bring about a change for good that would accomplish Your purposes.*

*Keep us safe, Father, and keep us always close to You.*

*Grant us Your strength and endurance for the battle—both physically and spiritually. May we abide in You for the duration of this wartime. Help us to stay the course, for we know that in due season we will reap a reward, if we do not lose heart (Galatians 6:9).*

*Forgive us for our many sins, Father, and help us to forgive the sins of others.*

*We ask all these things in Your precious, holy name.*

*AMEN.*

# A Prayer for Peace

When we are in the midst of conflict—especially long-standing conflict—peace almost seems unattainable. Yet, the *Holy Bible* speaks of a peace that surpasses all understanding. This peace can exist during conflict. This peace can live even when the entire world is crumbling around you, and you have nothing and no one to hold on to. This peace can be there when that knot at the end of your rope has somehow come undone. You can find God's strength, comfort and peace—even there.

Philippians 4:6-7 says this, "Don't worry about anything; instead, pray about everything. Tell God what you need, and thank him for all he has done. Then you will experience God's peace, which exceeds anything we can understand. His peace will guard your hearts and minds as you live in Christ Jesus."

Peace is not something that is effortless. It requires work on your part. Sometimes that work can be significant. In the Sermon on the Mount, recorded in the Fifth Chapter of Matthew, Jesus says, "God blesses those who work for peace, for they will be called the children of God" (Matthew 5:9).

Some people make peace seem completely out of reach, but we must humbly make every effort to be at peace with even the most difficult person in the world—the one that is 20 grit sandpaper on our skin, for the *Holy Bible* tells us, "If it is possible, as much as depends on you, live peaceably with all men" (Romans 12:18).

If we will keep our hearts and minds focused on trusting Christ, instead of ourselves, He will keep us in perfect peace, regardless of our circumstance.

"You will keep in perfect peace all who trust in you, all whose thoughts are fixed on you" (Isaiah 26:3)!

*Dear Father in Heaven,*

*You are the Prince of Peace. We thank You and praise You for Your awesome power and blessing in our life. We thank You for being mindful of us and for placing Your gentle hand of loving correction upon our lives in order to make us all that You would have us to be.*

*We come to You now with a request for peace. We are weary and exhausted with the conflict. We long for Your perfect peace—the peace that passes understanding, Father.*

*Help us to live peaceably with all men, Father. Show us just exactly what that means in this particular situation and in every situation to come. May we find strength in quietness and confidence and resting in You (Isaiah 30:15).*

*Lord, help us to be known as a peace-loving people. May we not be divisive, but may we remain true to You, allowing Your Word to penetrate our heart and spirit with wisdom.*

*We ask all these things in Your name.*
*AMEN.*

# A Prayer for Reconciliation

The task of reconciliation is often difficult—for everyone involved. The world tells us that there are many legitimate reasons to remain forever separated from each other—violations that are unforgivable. But God's Word says something different.

God wants us to follow His example, not the world's. He is an advocate of reconciliation, as in Hosea 3:1 when Hosea was reconciled to his wife, who had been unfaithful to him, "The Lord said to me, 'Go, show your love to your wife again, though she is loved by another and is an adulteress. Love her as the Lord loves the Israelites, though they turn to other gods and love the sacred raisin cakes.'"

The *Holy Bible* tells us that if we belong to Christ, we have become His ambassadors of reconciliation—reconciling all people to Him. 2 Corinthians 5:18-20 says, "All this is from God, who reconciled us to himself through Christ and gave us the ministry of reconciliation: that God was reconciling the world to himself in Christ, not counting men's sins against them. And he has committed to us the message of reconciliation. We are therefore Christ's ambassadors, as though God were making his appeal through us. We implore you on Christ's behalf: Be reconciled to God."

Reconciliation is not an easy task. It requires us to be forgiving, loving, gentle, kind, patient, peace-loving, joyful, and self-controlled—the fruits of the Spirit. We must be indwelled by Christ.

Christ has reconciled us to Himself, and we must be reconciled to others (Romans 5:11). Once we have been reconciled to Christ, then we are in a position to be reconciled to others.

When we are struggling in our efforts toward reconciliation, we can pray and ask God to help us.

*Dear Heavenly Father,*

*We thank You and praise You for reconciling us to You through Your son, Jesus Christ. We humbly ask You to forgive us for our sin and help us to forgive others who have wronged us.*

*Our heart is breaking for the separation we have with _____. Show us how to be reconciled to him/her/them.*

*Father, if there is anything separating us from You—any unconfessed sin—we ask that You reveal it to us that we may be reconciled to You.*

*Thank You for Your infinite love for us. Fill us with Your love for others. Erase the pain, Father. The hurt runs so very deep. It is so often overwhelming.*

*Help us to know when to speak and when to keep silent. Put words of peace and harmony in our hearts.*

*Give us victory in this situation, for we are so very weak in our own strength. We commit our every action, as well as the outcome, to You.*

*We ask all these things in Your perfect, holy name.*
*AMEN.*

# A Prayer for Restoration

When our lives have been damaged and torn apart by conflict, we long to be whole again. We long to have that missing element restored to us. Sometimes restoration is physical or financial. You may be looking for the restoration of a job, due to a wrongful termination. Or, the restoration you seek may be in the form of a relationship. Regardless the type of restoration you are seeking in your life, communication with God through prayer can and will help.

When we believe we have been unjustly wronged and are innocent of the consequences we are facing, our desire for restoration is greatest. The stories of restoration in the *Holy Bible* are many. God restored the cupbearer to his position with the king, after many days in prison with Joseph, in Genesis 40. There are also great stories of the restoration of Job, David, Isaiah, Hezekiah, Israel, Nehemiah, Ruth, Nebuchadnezzar and many more.

Truly the most spectacular story of restoration as a result of conflict is that of Jesus Christ. No one in the entire world experienced more conflict during His lifetime, and no one in all the world has been restored to greater position than Jesus Christ through his death, burial and resurrection. And, through Jesus Christ we, too, can experience His restoring power in every area of our lives.

I love what the *Holy Bible* says about restoration in 1 Peter 5:10, "In his kindness God called you to share in his eternal glory by means of Christ Jesus. So, after you have suffered a little while, he will restore, support, and strengthen you, and he will place you on a firm foundation."

There is no greater restoration than that of a firm foundation in Jesus Christ.

*Dear Heavenly Father,*

*Restore us unto You. Forgive us for our many sins, Father. We long to live a life that is pleasing to You.*

*Lord, we ask that You restore _____. We feel wronged and betrayed. We have so many emotions that well up inside. We need You to help us. Heal the hurt, Father.*

*Grant us patience in awaiting Your perfect plan of restoration in our lives. Give us peace in accepting Your perfect plan of restoration. Show us Your will and Your way.*

*Father, we pray that You would help us to be forgiving of others who have wronged us in this situation as You freely forgive us.*

*We thank You for the many examples of Your kind and loving restoration in the Holy Bible. We claim Your promise in Isaiah 54:7-8, "For a brief moment I abandoned you, but with great compassion I will take you back. In a burst of anger, I turned my face away for a little while. But with everlasting love I will have compassion on you," says the Lord, your Redeemer.*

*We thank you for your compassion. Restore to us the joy of Your salvation and make us willing to obey You (Psalm 51:12), Father.*

*In Your precious, holy name we pray.*
*AMEN.*

# A Prayer for Unity

When we are united in Christ, there is nothing that cannot be accomplished. The *Holy Bible* says, in Matthew 18:19-20, "I also tell you this: If two of you agree here on earth concerning anything you ask, my Father in heaven will do it for you. For where two or three gather together as my followers, I am there among them."

That is a powerful passage of Scripture. Read it again and allow every word to soak into your soul. The importance of unity cannot be minimized. For a nation, an army, a church, a school, a family or an individual to be effective, they must be united in their vision, their focus, and their purpose in Christ.

Ecclesiastes 4:12 says, "A person standing alone can be attacked and defeated, but two can stand back-to-back and conquer. Three are even better, for a triple-braided cord is not easily broken."

After Jesus ascended into heaven, there is a beautiful picture of unity among the early believers pictured in Acts 1:14, "They all met together and were constantly united in prayer, along with Mary the mother of Jesus, several other women, and the brothers of Jesus."

I love that verse. It is because of this unity in constant prayer that the body of believers grew from 120 to over 3,000 in one day at Pentecost! That is power. That is the power of prayer when we are united in Christ.

When we are in the thick of conflict and experiencing division, we can and should ask God to guide us to a place of unity in and through Him.

*Dear Heavenly Father,*

*Search me and know my heart; test me and know my anxious thoughts (Psalm 139:23). Show me any area of my life that is not totally devoted to You. May I be united in mind, body, and soul with Your purpose and Your will for every area of my life.*

*Pumice my heart and make it smooth. May I be united to this, Your body of believers.*

*Father, draw this entire body of believers together in unity to accomplish Your mission. Purge us of sin and selfishness. Grant us Your vision and Your focus, Father.*

*Lead us in Your ways.*

*Father, we commit ourselves to You afresh and anew. Fill us with Your love for others. May we always show Your love to each other.*

*Remove all conflict far from us, Heavenly Father.*

*We ask these things in Your precious, holy name.*

*AMEN.*

# A Prayer for Escape from Evil

Proverbs 15:3 says, "The Lord is watching everywhere, keeping his eye on both the evil and the good." Thank God, for He sees all things.

It can be extremely nerve-racking when we are pursued by evil, even though we are innocent and desire to be obedient to God. David felt this combination of fear, anger, injustice and frustration as he was hotly pursued by Saul, the father of his best friend, Jonathan.

When we are obedient to God, He honors that obedience. The *Holy Bible* says in Psalm 27:2, "When evil people come to devour me, when my enemies and foes attack me, they will stumble and fall." And, that is exactly what happened to Saul as he was overcome with evil in his attempt to destroy David. God made a way of escape from evil for David because of his obedience—because he longed to please God.

God provided David with Jonathan's friendship, and together they worked out a plan for David's protection (I Samuel 20). David hid in a cave awaiting Jonathan's signal as to whether or not Saul intended to kill David. When Jonathan learned that his father's heart was evil and intended only to kill David, he warned David by shooting arrows beyond a young boy's reach and calling out for him to "go farther". This told David that all was not well. So, David remained in hiding, and God made a way of escape for him.

God's protection and goodness towards those who are obedient to Him is boundless—especially in the face of evil. Psalm 91:7 says, "Though a thousand fall at your side, though ten thousand are dying around you, these evils will not touch you."

When you are surrounded by evil and feel as though there is no way of escape, God can make a way out for you, when no way out exists (I Corinthians 10:13). All we have to do is ask.

*Dear Heavenly Father,*

*I thank You that You make a way of escape in the face of evil. Please draw me close to You, and through Your divine power, enable me to escape this evil I am facing.*

*I praise You for what You are teaching me through this period of crisis. I thank You for lovingly providing protection for me.*

*Father, I can see Your hand of protection for me, and I claim Your promise in I Corinthians 10:13 that You will make a way of escape for me in the face of evil.*

*Lord, help me to see the beauty of Your justice, light, and power to overcome any and all obstacles in my life—obstacles that would otherwise hinder me from accomplishing Your purposes.*

*Continue to keep me firmly rooted and grounded in You, in Your Word, and in fellowship with other believers.*

*I ask all these things in Your most holy name.*
*AMEN.*

# A Prayer for Justice

Have you ever experienced a terrible wrong, or been unjustly accused and charged with wrongdoing when you were completely innocent? I have. It is a terribly helpless feeling—until we remember that the God who made the universe sees each tear we cry and loves us enough to know the number of hairs on our head (Matthew 10:30).

Many others have been wrongly accused and felt this way, too. Jesus is the greatest example. Another was Joseph. Joseph had been sold into slavery by his jealous brothers and made his way into the highest position in Potiphar's household. But Potiphar's wife did not have a heart that was right with God. She tried repeatedly to seduce him, but each time he refused to do wrong. In her wickedness and anger at being refused, Potiphar's wife accused Joseph of rape—when he had run from the house to get away from her (Genesis 39). Joseph was then thrown into prison for the crime.

Yet, God is just, and He sees all. In God's perfect timing, He used all the evil to accomplish His good purpose for Joseph's life. Joseph was eventually made ruler of Egypt! Only Pharaoh ranked above him.

Psalm 103:6 says, "The Lord gives righteousness and justice to all who are treated unfairly." I have always found this to be true in my own life, as well. Proverbs 21:15 says, "Justice is a joy to the godly, but it terrifies evildoers."

We also have a responsibility to others who are being mistreated or unjustly accused, to stand up for their cause and do what is right. Proverbs 31:8-9 says, "Speak up for those who cannot speak for themselves; ensure justice for those being crushed. Yes, speak up for the poor and helpless, and see that they get justice." When evil seems dominant and justice is hard to find, take heart. God is still in control.

*Dear Heavenly Father,*

*I love Your justice. Thank You for being the God of all justice. I praise You and thank You for allowing me to experience this period of injustice in order that You may be glorified when true justice finally prevails.*

*I ask that You bring about justice regarding _____.*

*Lord, help me to be steadfast in hope and faith in You. May I never falter. But, Father, if I do, please pick me back up and plant me on Your firm foundation of strength and righteousness.*

*I find it hard to wait for Your justice, Lord. Help me to wait. Allow me to be patient in hope, with the comfort of Your peace that passes all understanding.*

*Show me how to treat others justly, too, Father.*

*I ask all these things in Your perfect, holy name.*

*AMEN.*

# A Prayer for Dealing with a Fool

Have you ever experienced conflict with a foolish person? Chances are great that if you have lived for any length of time, you have. It is one of the most exasperating and unproductive of experiences to have any involvement with a foolish person.

Foolishness is the opposite of wisdom. The *Holy Bible* says a great deal about both wisdom and foolishness.

My favorite story on the subject is that of Nabal, Abigail, and David as recorded in I Samuel 25. Nabal was a very foolish man. In fact, the name Nabal means fool. Nabal was married to Abigail. The *Holy Bible* tells us that Abigail was a sensible and beautiful woman.

In the story, David and his men have moved to the wilderness of Maon near Carmel and encamped near the wealthy Nabal at the time of sheep-shearing. When David heard that Nabal was shearing his sheep, he sent some of his men to speak kindly to Nabal and ask for food in exchange for the kindness he had shown to Nabal's shepherds. David's men had acted as a shield for Nabal's shepherds—protecting them from harm and theft. Nabal responded in his typical, foolish fashion, refusing David's request and spouting off in anger. When David heard Nabal's response, he told his men to get their swords.

But Abigail was a wise woman. When she heard what her husband had done, she set to work immediately, sending a great deal of food to David and his men. When she encountered David, she bowed before him and acknowledged the foolishness of her husband and entreated David for forgiveness and mercy toward her household. David blessed Abigail and spared Nabal's household.

Upon learning what happened, Nabal had a stroke and was struck dead ten days later. When the news of Nabal's death reached David, he remembered Abigail and made her his wife.

Matthew 7:24-27 says, "Anyone who listens to my teaching and follows it is wise, like a person who builds a house on solid rock. Though the rain comes in torrents and the floodwaters rise and the winds beat against that house, it won't collapse because it is built on bedrock. But anyone who hears my teaching and doesn't obey it is foolish, like a person who builds a house on sand. When the rains and floods come and the winds beat against that house, it will collapse with a mighty crash."

You may have sung a song about this passage as a child in Sunday School. As an adult, it has even more meaning.

If you are struggling with conflict due to the behavior of one or more foolish people, prayer can help you. You can ask God to give you strength and guidance. He will not allow his righteous to be moved.

*Dear Heavenly Father,*

*Help me not to waste my breath on foolish people (Proverbs 23:9). Remind me, Father, that neither my time, money, nor energy need be spent on foolish people because they will return to their foolishness as a dog returning to its vomit (Proverbs 26:11).*

*But, Father, may I yet be filled with Your wisdom, and may it be enshrined in Your understanding (Proverbs 14:33).*

*I love Your discipline and correction, Father. I long to be brought into a place of total devotion and dependence upon You. Lord, we praise You for teaching us Your precepts and Your ways, for they lead only to life.*

*Give us patience, Father, and help us to guard our thoughts and our mouths when we encounter foolish people in the course of life. May we not give time or air to foolish conflicts in our life.*

*Forgive us for times when we have behaved foolishly. Keep us firmly planted in You at all times.*

*We ask all these things in Your perfect, holy name.*
*AMEN.*

# A Prayer for Courage

Are you embroiled in conflict and in need of courage today? The *Holy Bible* depicts courage brilliantly through the story of Ezra, the scribe, in the Old Testament book of Ezra.

After the Temple of the Lord had been rebuilt in Jerusalem, King Artaxerxes of Persia commissioned Ezra to conduct an inquiry into the current conditions in Judah and Jerusalem. The King decreed that anyone in the province may voluntarily return with Ezra to Jerusalem, and he was equipped with all manner of goods, including massive amounts of gold, silver, and bronze for the beautification of the Temple. Ezra praised God for His hand of favor and the goodness with which he had been treated by the king and all the nobles of the land.

However, the enemies of Judah and Jerusalem were many. Traveling with such great treasure could certainly have made Ezra and the other volunteers on the journey easy prey for enemies and bandits.

But the *Holy Bible* tells us in Ezra 8:21-23 what Ezra did before they continued their journey, "And there by the Ahava Canal, I gave orders for all of us to fast and humble ourselves before our God. We prayed that he would give us a safe journey and protect us, our children, and our goods as we traveled. For I was ashamed to ask the king for soldiers and horsemen to accompany us and protect us from enemies along the way. After all, we had told the king, 'Our God's hand of protection is on all who worship him, but his fierce anger rages against those who abandon him.' So, we fasted and earnestly prayed that our God would take care of us, and he heard our prayer."

God also heard the prayers of Moses, Joshua, David, Daniel, and many others in the *Holy Bible*. If you will humble yourself and have faith in Christ, He will hear you, too.

*Dear Heavenly Father,*

*We thank You that Your Word promises to restore the courage of those with repentant hearts (Isaiah 57:15).*

*We praise You for being the source of all courage, Lord.*

*We thank you that You are with us amid this struggle. May we lean completely and totally on You as our source of all strength and courage.*

*We ask that you forgive us for our sins, Father, and help us to turn from them.*

*Hear our prayer, and grant our request, Lord, for it is in Your Holy name we pray.*

*AMEN.*

# SECTION VI

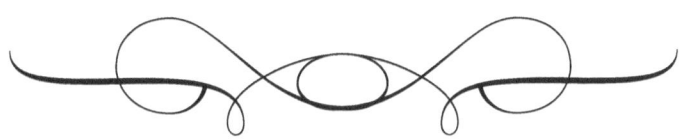

# Prayers
### for Times of
### Physical Need

# A Prayer for God's Provision

No matter what you need God to provide for you today, He is more than able. He owns the cattle on a thousand hills (Psalm 50:10). God's unfailing provision for us is depicted magnificently through the story of Abraham in Genesis 22.

At the beginning of the story, God calls to Abraham, saying, "Take your son, your only son—yes, Isaac, whom you love so much—and go to the land of Moriah. Go and sacrifice him as a burnt offering on one of the mountains, which I will show you."

Abraham did not hesitate. He saddled his donkey, took two of his servants along with his son, Isaac, and journeyed to Moriah. When they arrived, Isaac began to question his father, saying, "We have the fire and the wood, but where is the sheep for the sacrifice?" Abraham told his son that God would provide the sacrifice.

When, in obedience, Abraham prepared to offer his one and only son, God called to him and told him not to harm the boy. There in the thicket, a ram was caught by the horns. God provided for Abraham.

Listen to what God goes on to say to Abraham in Genesis 22:15-18, "Then the angel of the LORD called again to Abraham from heaven. 'This is what the LORD says: Because you have obeyed me and have not withheld even your son, your only son, I swear by my own name that I will certainly bless you. I will multiply your descendants beyond number, like the stars in the sky and the sand on the seashore. Your descendants will conquer the cities of their enemies. And through your descendants all the nations of the earth will be blessed—all because you have obeyed me.'"

The *Holy Bible* says, "To obey is better than sacrifice" (I Samuel 15:22). Simple childlike faith and obedience are pleasing to God. He does not require more of us than that.

Do you desire God's provision in your life today? Are you walking in faith and obedience to God? If so, He will provide for your every need and more.

*Dear Heavenly Father,*

*We need Your provision for our lives. Show us the way of obedience. Strengthen our faith. If there is an area in which we are being disobedient to You, Father, please reveal it to us, forgive us, and draw our hearts back home to You.*

*We thank You and praise You, Father, for being mindful of us, even more than a flock of sparrows (Matthew 10:31). We ask that You provide for us in every area of need, Father. We thank You for always providing for every need we have had in the past, and we thank You for Your continued provision in our lives.*

*Lord, keep us always close to You, and draw us away from the temptation to do wrong.*

*Show us how to give to others, Father. May we be cheerful givers—not stingy with our tithe to You. We thank You for the promise in Malachi 3:10, that if we will bring all the tithes into the storehouse, You will open the windows of heaven for us and pour out a blessing that is so great we won't have enough room to take it in!*

*Thank You for who You are, Father.*
*We ask all these things in Your precious, holy name.*
*AMEN.*

# A Prayer for Motivation to Work

There are a multitude of reasons for a person to become discouraged when in need of work. If you are discouraged and in need of motivation to work, God's Word offers hope, encouragement, and strength for you today.

Romans 12:11 says, "Never be lazy, but work hard and serve the Lord enthusiastically." Ephesians 6:7 says, "Work with enthusiasm, as though you were working for the Lord rather than for people." When we choose to work hard, despite the most difficult circumstances, we can be sure that God sees us, and He will reward us in ways we can never understand or imagine.

God has equipped each one of us with a special gift or ability that is necessary for the growth and development of everyone in the body of Christ. As Ephesians 4:16 tells us, "He makes the whole body fit together perfectly. As each part does its own special work, it helps the other parts grow, so that the whole body is healthy and growing and full of love."

Jesus served as the most excellent example of hard work for us as He served tirelessly both as a laborer in His youth and for the cause of the gospel, many times going without food in order to finish the Father's work.

Proverbs 21:5 says, "Good planning and hard work lead to prosperity, but hasty shortcuts lead to poverty."

The short and sweet fact of the matter is that our love for God and desire to please Him are motivating! When we act in obedience to Him, He sees and will reward us according to our actions; and, we will reap what we have sown—whether good or bad.

*Dear Heavenly Father,*

*We thank You for giving us the ability, motivation and the inspiration to work. We are often discouraged, Father. Help us to work as unto You, and not become discouraged. Help us to be diligent, encouraged, enthusiastic workers—excellent examples of Your light that lives within us, Lord.*

*Help us to commit to the work our hands find to do. May we find joy in the simple chores as well as the complex tasks of life.*

*Father, we pray that You would help us to be strong and quickly carry out the tasks assigned to us, for we know the night is coming when no one can work (John 9:4).*

*Lord, enable us to endure hardship as a good soldier (2 Timothy 2:3). Grant us the ability to endure troubles, hardships and calamities of every kind (2 Corinthians 6:4), without grumbling or complaining. Give us patience.*

*Fill us with Your Holy Spirit, Father, and wrap us in Your loving, strong embrace. Forgive us for our weakness, and may we forgive others in the same way that You forgive us.*

*We ask all these things in Your perfect, holy name.*
*AMEN.*

# A Prayer for Opportunity

Do you ever feel cursed? Do you feel as though some people receive more opportunity than they know what to do with, while you never seem to get a break? If you do, you are not alone. Job felt that way, too. In fact, he writes in Job 6:13, "No, I am utterly helpless, without any chance of success."

Job was experiencing a very difficult time in his life, and even his supposed friends kicked him when he was down. Job felt as though he had no opportunity to recover. Yet, after praying and pleading with God, things changed for Job.

Colossians 4:5 says, "Live wisely among those who are not believers, and make the most of every opportunity." We encounter opportunities for blessing every single day. Often these opportunities are disguised, or we do not make the most of them due to a lack of understanding.

In many cases, we do not suffer for a lack of opportunity. In many instances, it is our failure to act on the many opportunities we are given that causes crisis in our lives.

Whether we are suffering from a lack of opportunity, or a failure to take action on the opportunities given, communication with our Heavenly Father is key.

"Therefore, whenever we have the opportunity, we should do good to everyone—especially to those in the family of faith" (Galatians 6:10).

*Dear Heavenly Father,*

*Open our eyes to the opportunities around us. We thank You and praise You, Father for the many opportunities You provide. Help us to see them all. May we take advantage of and make the most of every opportunity we encounter.*

*Father, help us to seize the day, rejoicing in what we have, rather than the things we are lacking. Lord, today we choose to do good to all in every opportunity we are given.*

*Guard us and protect us from the evil one, Heavenly Father. Remind us that You are always with us.*

*We are in awe, Father, that You are mindful of us. We ask, specifically, that You would provide us with an opportunity to _____.*

*You are the giver of all good things, both in Heaven and in Earth.*

*We thank You and praise You for the opportunity to give back to You.*

*In Your most precious name, we pray.*

*AMEN.*

# A Prayer for Shelter

In the Old Testament, the Israelites observed a seven-day celebration in early autumn called the Festival of Shelters. This festival was held to remind the people of their rescue from Egypt, and how the Lord provided shelters for all of the homeless Israelites to live in—even as they wandered.

Are you wandering and in need of shelter? God wants to remind you that He is there for you, too. Psalm 36:7 says, "How precious is your unfailing love, O God! All humanity finds shelter in the shadow of your wings."

The promises for you in the *Holy Bible* concerning shelter are so many. Psalm 61:4 says, "Let me live forever in your sanctuary, safe beneath the shelter of your wings!"

Psalm 91:4 says, "He will cover you with his feathers. He will shelter you with his wings. His faithful promises are your armor and protection."

If you are in need of shelter today, let God be your shelter. Bring your request to Him in prayer. He will supply all your needs, as His Word promises in Philippians 4:19, "And this same God who takes care of me will supply all your needs from his glorious riches, which have been given to us in Christ Jesus."

The *Holy Bible* tells us in Matthew 8:20, "But Jesus replied, 'Foxes have dens to live in, and birds have nests, but the Son of Man has no place even to lay his head.'"

If you are homeless and in need of shelter, Jesus understands. He's been right where you are. There is none more loving, understanding, or more receptive to your need than Him.

*Dear Heavenly Father,*

*We thank You for the shelter You provide us through Your never-ending love for us. You surround us in the shelter of Your wings and hold us close to You. How we praise You, Father!*

*Father, You know that we are in need of an earthly dwelling place. We come to You because You understand our need. You have been where we are. We thank You and praise You for being able to provide for every aspect of our being. We praise You for the joy You are teaching us through this difficult time.*

*Father, we thank You for teaching us to totally depend upon You for everything. Guide us in our actions. May we be diligent to do the things You call us to do to bring about shelter for ourselves, our families and others who are in need of the same thing.*

*Forgive us for failing to trust You at all times. We thank You for Your promise in James 1:17, that "Whatever is good and perfect comes down to us from God our Father, who created all the lights in the heavens. He never changes or casts a shifting shadow."*

*We receive Your love and blessing into our lives today.*
*In Jesus name we pray.*
*AMEN.*

# A Prayer for Food

Jesus prayed, "Give us today the food we need," in Matthew 6:11. When we find ourselves hungry and in need of food, we must ask.

David tells us in Psalm 37:25, "I was young and now I am old, yet I have never seen the righteous forsaken or their children begging bread." God takes care of the needs of those who follow after Him.

But, if you are a child of God, you have a responsibility to be His hands and feet—to meet the needs of others around you. Do you have enough food for your household? If so, you are commanded to give liberally to those in need! Luke 6:38 tells us, "Give, and it will be given to you. A good measure, pressed down, shaken together and running over, will be poured into your lap. For with the measure you use, it will be measured to you." If there is enough food in your house for today, have an attitude of gratitude.

Matthew 6:34 reminds us, "So don't worry about tomorrow, for tomorrow will bring its own worries. Today's trouble is enough for today."

The same God, who fed a crowd of over five thousand people with a young boy's gift of five loaves of bread and two fish, can meet your need today. The God who made food called manna rain down from Heaven to feed the Israelites as they left captivity in Egypt—the one who owns the cattle on a thousand hills—has more than enough food for you today.

Ask Him to meet your need.

*Dear Heavenly Father,*

*We pray as You taught us by example, to give us this day our daily bread. We know that You have more than enough power and provision to meet our need. We ask that You divinely intervene in our circumstance and provide food for us to eat and clean water for us to drink this day.*

*Thank You for providing for us day and night throughout our entire lives. Forgive us for not always having an attitude of gratitude, Father, for You are worthy of our praise at all times, Lord.*

*Thank You for the many examples of Your faithfulness that You provide to us in Your Word. Keep us always mindful of Your goodness and mercy toward us.*

*We praise You for hearing and answering our prayer and providing the food and drink we need for this day, Father.*

*It is in Your perfect, holy name that we ask these things.*

*AMEN.*

# A Prayer for Employment

Ecclesiastes 9:10 says, "Whatever you do, do well. For when you go to the grave, there will be no work or planning or knowledge or wisdom." There is always work that needs to be done. Yet, often our circumstances present a unique desire for employment at a certain income level, training level, specific schedule or location.

The God who created the universe and still sets the captives free is big enough to handle any need we have—even the need for specific employment. But there is a caution before taking any such request before our Heavenly Father. We must be certain of the purity of our motivation.

Proverbs 16:2 reminds us, "People may be pure in their own eyes, but the Lord examines their motives." If we are God's children, then we must serve Him in EVERYTHING we do. Keeping service to Him and hard work for Him as our goal, our need for employment will most assuredly be met.

"And this same God who takes care of me will supply all your needs from his glorious riches, which have been given to us in Christ Jesus" (Philippians 4:19).

When Abraham was old, he sent his oldest servant on a mission to find a Godly wife for his son, Isaac. Listen to the servant's prayer in Genesis 24:12, "O Lord, God of my master, Abraham," he prayed. "Please give me success today, and show unfailing love to my master, Abraham." God heard the servant's prayer and granted him success in the mission his master had given to him.

When your heart is right and you make your request known to God through prayer, He will grant you success, too.

*Dear Heavenly Father,*

*We thank You for the many opportunities we have in our world to work. Open our eyes, our minds, and our hearts to the endless possibilities for service to You.*

*Father, we ask that You grant us success in finding the employment You desire for us. Give us a clear sense of Your direction and purpose for our life's work.*

*Lord, we ask specifically for _____.*

*Thank You for hearing and answering our prayer. We thank You for the promise in Your Word that if we delight ourselves in You, Father, You will grant us the desires of our heart. We claim this promise and seek You and Your will with our whole heart, Lord.*

*May Your name be praised and glorified forevermore.*

*In Your precious, holy name we pray.*

*AMEN.*

# A Prayer for Clothing

In Luke 12, Jesus taught His disciples about God's goodness and care for them with regard to the need for clothing.

Luke 12:27-28 says, "Look at the lilies and how they grow. They don't work or make their clothing, yet Solomon in all his glory was not dressed as beautifully as they are. And if God cares so wonderfully for flowers that are here today and thrown into the fire tomorrow, he will certainly care for you. Why do you have so little faith?"

Are you worried about having the proper clothing to wear today? This passage tells us clearly that God loves us much more than enough to meet this need in our lives today.

Do you trust God to meet this need? If you are struggling with a lack of faith that God could or should love you enough to meet this need, you can take your struggle to Him in prayer today.

God loves us so much that He desires to meet our every need (Philippians 4:19). Even when the Israelites wandered in the wilderness for forty years after their disobedience to the will of God, He met their need for clothing.

Nehemiah 9:21 tells us, "Forty years You sustained them in the wilderness; They lacked nothing; Their clothes did not wear out and their feet did not swell."

If you are worrying about the need for clothing, you are not relinquishing control to your Heavenly Father. Take it all to the Lord in prayer.

*Dear Heavenly Father,*

*We give our need for clothing to You, asking You and trusting You to surely meet this need. We thank You and praise You, Precious Father, for meeting every need we have ever had.*

*Increase our faith, Father. Help us not to waiver, for You prove Yourself faithful to us in all things.*

*We thank You for the love You exhibit in disciplining us, Father.*

*Thank You for providing beautiful clothing for us to wear. May we give to others in need, as well. Help us to share with all we find in need.*

*Forgive us for failing to meet the needs of others. Remove all selfishness from our lives. May we forever cling to You.*

*In Your precious, holy name we pray.*
AMEN.

# A Prayer Regarding Finances

The *Holy Bible* teaches us a great deal about money. Our handling of and dealing with money is a direct indication of our overall spiritual well-being—a barometer for the condition of our soul.

Hebrews 13:5 says, "Don't love money; be satisfied with what you have. For God has said, "I will never fail you. I will never abandon you."

Many of us improperly manage our finances, and due to our sin or the sin of a family member, we find ourselves in difficult circumstances. However, God loves us so much that He meets us at our point of need, and He commands us to do the same for others. 1 John 3:17 says, "If someone has enough money to live well and sees a brother or sister in need but shows no compassion—how can God's love be in that person?"

God has a desire for us to be obedient to Him, and in that obedience is the richness and blessing of all that He has made. Tithing is an important part of our obedience to Him. A tithe is one-tenth of everything we receive.

God loves us so much more than our minds can comprehend, and He even tells us to test Him when it comes to our finances! Malachi 3:10 says, "Bring all the tithes into the storehouse so there will be enough food in my Temple. If you do," says the Lord of Heaven's Armies, "I will open the windows of heaven for you. I will pour out a blessing so great you won't have enough room to take it in! Try it! Put me to the test!"

Are you struggling in your finances today? Have faith in God. Allow Him to prove his faithfulness to you and put His Word to the test.

*Dear Heavenly Father,*

*We are struggling with our finances. Specifically, we need _____ _____.*

We thank You, Father, and praise You for meeting our needs. Lord, Your blessings are too many to count. We humbly ask that You teach us to be faithful to You in our giving. May we always be cheerful and generous givers, reflecting the manner in which we receive from You (2 Corinthians 9:7).

Father, help us to live out Your Word, as it is written in Luke 6:38, "Give, and you will receive. Your gift will return to you in full—pressed down, shaken together to make room for more, running over, and poured into your lap. The amount you give will determine the amount you get back."

We thank You and praise You for being more than able to meet our need. Thank You for bending down and hearing our prayer and meeting our need.

May we be always faithful and ever mindful of Your love and grace toward us.

We ask all these things in Your precious, holy name.

AMEN.

# A Prayer for Favorable Weather

"He causes the clouds to rise over the whole earth. He sends the lightning with the rain and releases the wind from his storehouses" (Psalm 135:7).

Perhaps you've heard about how God allowed the Israelites to cross the Red Sea on dry land as they left their captivity in the land of Egypt. Did you know that God did this by causing a strong east wind to blow across the sea? The wind blew all night, turning the seabed into dry land (Exodus 14:21)!

The *Holy Bible* also tells us about the Prophet Elijah—a man who was just as human as you and me. Elijah prayed earnestly for no rain to fall, and for three-and-a-half years, no rain fell in the land of Israel during King Ahab's reign. Then, when Elijah prayed again, the sky sent forth its rain and the ground began to yield its crops again!

Do you remember the story of Jesus sleeping in a boat when a fierce storm arose? The disciples quickly rushed to wake Jesus, asking Him to save them for they were afraid they would drown. Jesus responded in Matthew 8:26, "Jesus responded, "Why are you afraid? You have so little faith!" Then He got up and rebuked the wind and waves, and suddenly there was a great calm. The disciples were in awe, wondering who this was that truly had the power to make the wind and the waves obey Him.

Are you burdened with unpleasant, difficult weather? I know the One who set the earth in motion and commands the clouds to churn about at His direction (Job 37:12).

"If he commands it, the sun won't rise and the stars won't shine" (Job 9:7).

Take your request to Him in prayer.

*Dear Heavenly Father,*

*We thank You for commanding the weather that is in Your power, control, and sovereign direction. We are amazed that You are mindful of even how the weather affects us, Father. Please hear our prayer and answer our plea for favorable weather.*

*Father, we know You are a God of justice and righteousness. In Your righteousness, please grant our request for _____.*

*Father, You know our need before we ask. Yet, Your Word reminds us to ask, seek and knock that You may give, we may find, and the door shall be opened unto us (Matthew 7:7-8). We thank You that Your Word is true. And, we thank You that Your Word tells us that the wind and weather obey You (Psalm 148:8).*

*Please hear our cry and answer our prayer to You this day, Father, for we continue in obedience to You. It is our desire to be pleasing to You, Father.*

*And, it is in Your perfect, holy name we pray.*
*AMEN.*

# A Prayer for Helping Hands

"Give me a helping hand, for I have chosen to follow your commandments" (Psalm 119:173).

Each of us needs helping hands at some point and time in our lives. That is the way that God created us. He wants us to fellowship with one another and to bear each other's burdens.

My father has always been an excellent example to me of someone who offers his hands to help others in need. As a young girl, I remember many times when my father was not home because someone needed a helping hand in painting their house or mending a broken porch step. He always felt an urgency to help those in need of assistance when it was within his power to do so.

But what if you are that person in need of assistance? How do you gain access to those helping hands—the helping hands of God in your life?

The *Holy Bible* tells us that when our walk is blameless and our hearts are seeking after God in all things, we can pray to God and ask Him to save those who are in trouble, and He will help them (Job 22:29).

Ezra 8:23 says, "So we fasted and earnestly prayed that our God would take care of us, and he heard our prayer."

God can and will do the same for you.

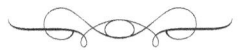

*Dear Heavenly Father,*

*We humbly bow before You, thanking You for Your unfailing grace, mercy and love for us. We ask that You forgive us for our many failures.*

*Lord, we need Your hands to help us today. We ask specifically, for Your help in _____. We thank You for hearing our prayer, Father, and for answering in accordance with Your mighty power.*

*We praise You for constantly caring for us and for our every need.*

*Strengthen us in our weakness, Father, and guide us in Your path of light. Give us opportunity to be Your helping hands and feet to others who are in need. May we always show Your abundant love to everyone we meet.*

*Thank You, Father, for helping hands that have rescued me in days past.*

*It is in Your precious name we pray.*

*AMEN.*

# SECTION VII

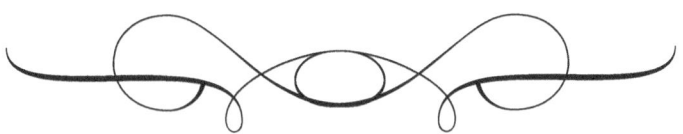

# Prayers
### for Times of Despair

# A Prayer for Hope

"Let all that I am wait quietly before God, for my hope is in him" (Psalm 62:5).

Horatio Gates Spafford was a wealthy lawyer and businessman who invested much of his money in Chicago real estate in the late 1800s. In 1871, when the great Chicago fire occurred, Horatio and his family lost almost everything. About that same time, Horatio and his wife, Anna, lost their one and only son. They had four daughters. Yet, despite his own tragedy, Spafford and his wife spent many hours assisting the other victims of the Chicago fire.

Not long after that, Horatio Spafford and his family were traveling to Europe for an evangelistic crusade and vacation. Horatio was detained by business but sent his family ahead by ship. The ship collided with another, and sank within twenty minutes, taking Horatio Spafford's four daughters to their death. Only his wife, Anna, one of 47 survivors, remained.

Soon after this tragedy, Horatio Gates Spafford penned the famous hymn, *It Is Well with My Soul*. The hymn epitomizes our hope in Jesus Christ—no matter what manner of despair we face in this life. We have an eternal hope in Jesus Christ.

Horatio Spafford and his wife moved to Jerusalem, Israel ten years after the great Chicago fire, with two daughters God saw fit to bless them with. They helped to start a group called the American Colony, whose mission was to help the poor.[1]

Is your life going a bit like Horatio Spafford's? Are you feeling desperate? Are you feeling despair? Remember that God's Word offers hope for times of despair.

Romans 5:5 reminds us of that with these words, "And hope does not disappoint us, because God has poured out his love into our hearts by the Holy Spirit, whom he has given us."

---

[1] See Nobel prize winning *Jerusalem* by Swedish novelist Selma Lagerlöf.

*Dear Heavenly Father,*

*We bow before You with thanksgiving and pray as the Psalmist prayed, "You faithfully answer our prayers with awesome deeds, O God our savior. You are the hope of everyone on earth, even those who sail on distant seas." (Psalm 65:5)*

*Father, our circumstances have brought us to the pit of darkest despair. Please reach down and pick us up from this lowly state and renew our hope in You alone.*

*We trust in Your Word, Father, and we ask that You remind us of Your glorious plan. We thank You and praise You that we are a part of this glorious plan You have.*

*Dear Lord, we commit afresh and anew to placing 100% of our hope and trust in You. We thank You that the hopes of the godly result in happiness (Proverbs 10:28). We praise You for blessing those whose hope and confidence lie in You (Jeremiah 17:7).*

*We thank You and praise You, Heavenly Father, that Your hope is a strong and trustworthy anchor for our souls that leads us through the curtain into God's inner sanctuary (Hebrews 6:19).*

*May we dwell secure in this hope forever, for it is in Your precious, holy name we pray.*

*AMEN.*

# A Prayer when Tempted by Suicide

If you are reading this now and contemplating suicide, you have reached the pinnacle of despair. I don't know what has brought you to this place, but God does. And, believe it or not, He still has a plan for your life—in the midst of your desperation, pain, hurt, and desire to end the beautiful life He has given to you. He will never stop loving you.

He is the way to life. In your temptation to commit such a final act, remember that countless people have felt the desperation you feel right now. Countless people are feeling desperate along with you right now.

David was one man in the *Holy Bible* who felt this same desperation. He had many troubles—some he had brought upon himself, some he had not. Here is what David said in Psalm 34:6, "In my desperation I prayed, and the LORD listened; he saved me from all my troubles."

The Lord can do the same for you. Would you please pray with me?

*Dear Heavenly Father,*

*I am feeling such a deep since of pain and despair that I cannot bear it any longer. I give my feelings of pain, despair, and suicide to You. I lay them at Your feet.*

*Father, I give you all of my burdens and cares because I know that You care for me (I Peter 5:7).*

*I thank You that You have a plan for my life here on earth that is a plan to prosper me and not to bring disaster. It is a plan to give hope and a future (Jeremiah 29:11).*

*Father, help me to have the faith to believe that—and to act upon it—one hour at a time, one day at a time.*

*Forgive me, Father, for doubting Your love for me. Draw me close to You, and remove the evil one far from my mind, body, spirit and emotions. Help me to forgive others who continue to hurt me.*

*I praise You for Your infinite love for me and ask all these things in Your holy name.*

*AMEN.*

# A Prayer for Love

Are you feeling unloved? Or, perhaps you are being treated as though you are unlovable. Maybe you just *feel* unloved or unlovable.

May I say to you that there is someone who loves you right now, and that His love is so far-reaching you cannot escape it. In fact, His love is so strong that there is nothing we can do or say that will make Him stop loving us.

He is the definition of love itself. Without Him, all other love is incomplete. There is nowhere we can go where His love cannot reach down and carry us, hold us, wrap around us.

The *Holy Bible* says in Romans 8:38-39, "And I am convinced that nothing can ever separate us from God's love. Neither death nor life, neither angels nor demons, neither our fears for today nor our worries about tomorrow—not even the powers of hell can separate us from God's love. No power in the sky above or in the earth below—indeed, nothing in all creation will ever be able to separate us from the love of God that is revealed in Christ Jesus our Lord."

Human love fails. We are weak and we all sin. But God has a love that endures forever. Are you in need of this kind of love today?

You can pray and ask God to help you to receive His love.

*O, Father in Heaven,*

*Your unfailing love is better than life itself; how I praise You (Psalm 63:3)! How we need Your love! We thank You, O God, that Your love is always and forever surrounding and abounding toward us.*

*Help us to receive that love and to give it back to everyone we meet, unconditionally. Help us to love the unlovable including ourselves, Father. We thank You that You ARE love personified! We praise You for allowing us to commune with You—to have a personal relationship with You, Father.*

*Work Your perfect will in our lives, Lord, and bring other people into our lives who are in need of Your love. Give us the ability to show Your love to them, Father. May we love our neighbors as ourselves, Father. Help us to act in a manner that would point all mankind to You.*

*Forgive us when we fail in this attempt, Lord, and grant us endurance for this lifelong journey. Help me to be a committed rather than a casual Christian.*

*We ask all these things in Your precious, holy name.*
*AMEN.*

# A Prayer for Deliverance

"For I know that as you pray for me and the Spirit of Jesus Christ helps me, this will lead to my deliverance" (Philippians 1:19).

There are many accounts in the *Holy Bible* of despair and deliverance. The key to unlocking the door of deliverance is faith. We must believe that God stands ready, willing and able to deliver us and meet us at our point of need. And, we must believe that He will deliver.

In my life, I can attest that God has always met me at my point of need. He has always delivered me—in every possible way imaginable. And, in each instance, God has used whatever trouble I have encountered to draw me ever closer to Him.

The *Holy Bible* says in Psalm 40:2, "He lifted me out of the pit of despair, out of the mud and the mire. He set my feet on solid ground and steadied me as I walked along."

God is ready to deliver you from the pit of despair. He is ready to set your feet on solid ground—to steady you as you walk.

No matter how big the mountain, God can help you climb it. As God delivered the Israelites from the land of Egypt, He stands ready to deliver you today.

2 Corinthians 1:9-11 tells us, "Indeed, in our hearts we felt the sentence of death. But this happened that we might not rely on ourselves but on God, who raises the dead. He has delivered us from such a deadly peril, and he will deliver us. On him we have set our hope that he will continue to deliver us, as you help us by your prayers. Then many will give thanks on our behalf for the gracious favor granted us in answer to the prayers of many."

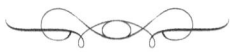

*Dear Heavenly Father,*

*O, how we need Your deliverance! Help us, Father, to depend completely and totally upon You as the source of our strength. We thank You for Your ability to deliver us. We ask that You strengthen our faith, Father, and help us in our weakness.*

*Lord, we believe that You will deliver _____ from _____.
We know that it is Your desire to set the captives free (Isaiah 61:1).*

*We thank You for delivering us out of the pit of despair in times past. We do not want to be enslaved by sin. We praise You for the freedom that comes from knowing and trusting in You (Romans 6:14).*

*We delight in Your Word and hunger for more of it constantly. We thank You for Your law of love.*

*Help us, O Lord, to find Your deliverance in all things.*

*In Jesus precious name we pray.*

*AMEN.*

# A Prayer for Laughter

The book of Ecclesiastes reminds us that there is a time for every purpose under Heaven. There is "a time to cry and a time to laugh" (Ecclesiastes 3:4).

When we feel in the depths of despair, it is often hard to remember what laughter felt like. As Proverbs 14:13 says, "Laughter can conceal a heavy heart, but when the laughter ends, the grief remains."

Have you experienced that verse? Do you long for the despair and heaviness of your heart to dissipate? Job did, too. He was a man of integrity. He feared and loved God, yet he was suffering in the worst way.

In the midst of Job's pain and despair, he was able to remind us of God's infinite mercy and goodness toward us.

Job 8:21 says, "He will once again fill your mouth with laughter and your lips with shouts of joy."

If you long for laughter to return to your life, you can ask God for it.

Luke 6:21 tells us, "God blesses you who are hungry now, for you will be satisfied. God blesses you who weep now, for in due time you will laugh."

In God's perfect timing, you will laugh again.

*Dear Heavenly Father,*

*How we long for sweet laughter to return to our lips and to our heart. We praise You that we have known laughter in days past. We thank You for the sorrow and despair we experience, for we know that through it all You are working about Your perfect, precious, and merciful will in our lives.*

*Help us to return from the pit of despair and know the true joy, happiness, peace, and, yes, laughter that can only come by knowing and serving You completely.*

*Forgive us for dwelling on our own circumstance and not looking to the needs of others. May we truly be Your servants in everything we say and do, Father.*

*We ask all these things in Your precious, holy name.*
AMEN.

# A Prayer to Overcome Bitterness

Bitterness is a poison. When we allow it to take root in our lives, it is a destructive force that rips and tears at the very foundation of our soul. If we find bitterness developing in those around us, the *Holy Bible* tells us that we are to lovingly encourage them and draw them back into the fullness of God's grace.

Hebrews 12:15 tells us, "Look after each other so that none of you fails to receive the grace of God. Watch out that no poisonous root of bitterness grows up to trouble you, corrupting many."

Ephesians 4:31 says, "Get rid of all bitterness, rage, anger, harsh words, and slander, as well as all types of evil behavior."

As I was growing up, my father always had a great cure for bitterness—both in himself and in others. It was called service. Whenever he felt a root of bitterness sneaking into his life due to the devastating pressures and circumstances of life, he would find someone who needed his help, and he would give what he had to help them.

The gift of his service didn't change his circumstances, but it did change the attitude with which he experienced those circumstances. Suddenly and miraculously, the bitterness was gone.

Is bitterness threatening you? Have you allowed bitterness to take root in your life and grow into a destructive force? Prayer can help you to overcome the devastating effects of bitterness in your life, your heart, your soul.

*Dear Heavenly Father,*

*You know our hearts. You know all things. Please remove bitterness that has taken root in my life and has begun to destroy me. Father, You know the actions and attitudes in my heart that have caused this. Change me, Father. Restore me unto You and create in me a clean heart (Psalm 51:10).*

*Thank you, Lord, for the gift of Your grace. Help me to receive it. Help me to turn away from the tendency to dwell on negative thoughts. May I find Your goodness, grace and love in serving others.*

*We thank You and praise You for Your many blessings. We commit today to changing our way of thinking, Father. We commit to dwelling on all things true, right, lovely, pure, admirable, and heavenly (Romans 8:5, Philippians 4:8, Colossians 3:2) in order to be pleasing to Your Holy Spirit.*

*We ask that You help us, Father. We thank You for sending Your Holy Spirit as a comforter to help us in our time of need. Forgive us for our many failures.*

*We ask all these things in Your precious, holy name.*
*AMEN.*

# A Prayer when a Job Is Lost

Whether the job was lost due to your own fault or no fault of your own, it can be a stressful time—begging every last ounce of faith in God's plan of provision for your life and those dependent upon you.

There is something to be said for the personal satisfaction that comes from a job well done. Galatians 6:4 tells us, "Pay careful attention to your own work, for then you will get the satisfaction of a job well done, and you won't need to compare yourself to anyone else."

Do you ever do that? Do you compare yourself to others and how much they are able to produce financially? The *Holy Bible* warns us against that way of thinking, and reminds us in Matthew 6:33 to, "But seek first his kingdom and his righteousness, and all these things will be given to you as well."

If you have lost employment due to no fault of your own, perhaps God is closing one door in preparation for a new opportunity that is opening in your life—a new opportunity for growth and blessing. "Commit to the LORD whatever you do, and your plans will succeed" (Proverbs 16:3).

If you have lost employment due to your own foolishness or poor behavior, then God can also use this as a point of growth and blessing in your life. Ecclesiastes 11:6 tells us, "Sow your seed in the morning, and at evening let not your hands be idle, for you do not know which will succeed, whether this or that, or whether both will do equally well."

*Dear Heavenly Father,*

*We are in distress due to a lost job. Please bless the work of our hands, Lord, and help us to find work. We commit our work to You.*

*Lord, we ask that You open the door of employment that You would have us pass through. We pray that You would close all other doors.*

*Teach us what You would have us to learn from this difficult time. Help us to have a teachable heart, Father.*

*And, Lord, may our hands work with all our might at whatever they find to do that we may be pleasing to You (Ecclesiastes 9:10).*

*Father, draw us ever closer to You. Forgive us for becoming cold and hardened. Soften our hearts to the needs of others. Help us to be the servant You have called us to be.*

*We ask all these things in Your perfect, precious, and holy name.*
*AMEN.*

# A Prayer when You've Had a Great Fall

Do you remember this well-known nursery rhyme?

HUMPTY DUMPTY[2]

Humpty Dumpty sat on a wall,
Humpty Dumpty had a great fall.
All the king's horses, and all the king's men,
Couldn't put Humpty together again.

Perhaps all the king's horses and all the king's men couldn't put Humpty together again, but God can. When we give Him all the broken pieces of our life, He can put us back together—better than we were before.

Have you fallen so hard you feel as though there is no way you can possibly get back up? Psalm 145:14 says, "The Lord helps the fallen and lifts those bent beneath their loads."

If I were re-writing Humpty Dumpty to show what God can do for you, it would go something like this:

HUMPTY DUMPTY

Humpty Dumpty sat on a wall,
Humpty Dumpty had a great fall.
All of God's grace, His love and compassion,
Put Humpty together in glorious fashion.

Psalm 147:3 says, "He heals the brokenhearted and bandages their wounds." Give God all the broken pieces of your life today, and He will put you back together in glorious fashion, too.

---

2 Original author unknown.

*Dear Heavenly Father,*

*I have fallen. I need Your help to get back up again. I can't make it on my own, Lord. I need You every day, every hour, every second of my life. Thank You for loving me. Forgive me for my disobedience, Father.*

*Guard me against the attacks of the enemy. Purge me of my sin and restore me to a right standing and favor with You, Heavenly Father. I long to return to You and be kept in Your safe dwelling place.*

*Pick me back up, Father. Thank You for hearing me when I call on You. Rescue me, Father. Lift me up and place me back on solid ground.*

*You are all I need in this world, Father. I praise You because You will never leave me or forsake me.*

*Please put me back together again—better than I was before.*

*In Jesus precious name I pray.*

*AMEN.*

# A Prayer when Facing Prison Time

Once upon a time, there was a beautiful, wonderful, and precious child born out of God's divine plan. That child was, and still is, you.

I don't know why you are facing a prison sentence, but you and God know. Search your heart and soul. Ask yourself why this has happened.

Now, take the time to get down on your knees and ask God how your life can be used in this situation to bring glory and honor to Him. He can change things. He can take the worst situation imaginable and turn it into all things glorious.

Isaiah 61:3 says, "To all who mourn in Israel, he will give a crown of beauty for ashes, a joyous blessing instead of mourning, festive praise instead of despair. In their righteousness, they will be like great oaks that the Lord has planted for his own glory."

Joseph was imprisoned in the *Holy Bible*, based on the false witness of his employer's wife. Yet, in spite of the horrific pain this surely caused him, Joseph found a way to do good to others. He continued to prove that he was responsible—a man of impeccable character. Genesis 39:21 tells us, "But the Lord was with Joseph in the prison and showed him his faithful love. And the Lord made Joseph a favorite with the prison warden."

The most well-known prisoner in the *Holy Bible* was Jesus. Yet, He never once committed any sin. He has experienced what you are experiencing now. He was beaten and broken for you. But Jesus' heart and mind were set on things above. He was focused—not on Himself or His circumstance—but on serving the needs of others and showing His Heavenly Father's love to them . . . even in prison.

*Dear Heavenly Father,*

*Help me to honor You, even as I face this prison term. Thank You for allowing this to happen to me that You may make me into the person You want me to become. Replace my cold, stone heart with a new heart—a heart that is soft and tender as a newborn child.*

*Help me, Father, to focus on how I can help others. Use me to make a positive difference in the lives of others in this prison.*

*Change me, Father. Smooth off the many rough spots of my character. I commit my life to serving You. Guide me in Your way.*

*Forgive me, Lord, for the many wrongs I have committed against You and others. Help me to forgive others for their wrongs against me, just as You forgive me.*

*Work a miracle in my life, Father. I believe You can, and I believe You will.*

*In Your precious, holy name I pray.*

AMEN.

# A Prayer when Severely Depressed

Difficult circumstances can lead any of us to the point of depression. Consider the depression experienced by Jesus prior to His crucifixion in Matthew 26:36-38, "Then Jesus went with them to the olive grove called Gethsemane, and he said, 'Sit here while I go over there to pray.' He took Peter and Zebedee's two sons, James and John, and he became anguished and distressed. He told them, 'My soul is crushed with grief to the point of death. Stay here and keep watch with me.'"

King David prayed in Psalm 143:7, "Come quickly, Lord, and answer me, for my depression deepens. Don't turn away from me, or I will die."

Job cries out to God in Job 7:16, "I hate my life and don't want to go on living. Oh, leave me alone for my few remaining days."

Is that the kind of depression you are facing today? Do you feel as though you could die? If so, prayer to the one true and living God can help you. Through prayer and faith in Christ, you can be brought back from severe depression and despair, experiencing the comfort that the Holy Spirit provides.

Job, David and Jesus experienced depression and despair, but each of their stories went far beyond depression and despair to victory. You can experience that same victory.

I John 5:4 reminds us, "For every child of God defeats this evil world, and we achieve this victory through our faith."

*Dear Heavenly Father,*

*We draw near to You and ask for relief from this overwhelming depression we face. Come quickly to rescue us, Lord! We long for Your mercy, grace, love, and favor in our lives!*

*We thank You and praise You, Father, for You rescue us (Psalm 13:5)!*

*Remind us of Your many miracles that we may rejoice in the faith that You will again bring about miraculous works in and through our own lives.*

*We humbly submit to Your loving discipline in our lives, Lord.*

*Strengthen our faith and anticipation of the good works that are consistent with Your character.*

*Keep us always from the pit of despair, and guard us from depression. And, Father, may this experience bring honor and glory to Your name always.*

*In Your precious name, we pray.*
*AMEN.*

# Section VIII

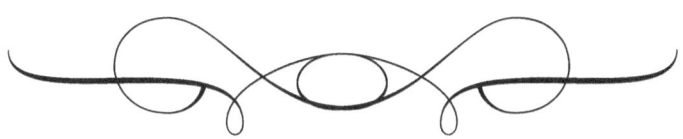

rayers
*for* Times *of* Loneliness

# A Prayer for Companionship

When God made Adam, He recognized that it was not good for Adam to be alone. That is why God made Eve—to be a companion. God does not want us to live our lives in isolation. He wants us to enjoy companionship.

Ecclesiastes 4:9-12 talks about some other reasons why companionship is important, "Two people are better off than one, for they can help each other succeed. If one person falls, the other can reach out and help. But someone who falls alone is in real trouble. Likewise, two people lying close together can keep each other warm. But how can one be warm alone? A person standing alone can be attacked and defeated, but two can stand back-to-back and conquer. Three are even better, for a triple-braided cord is not easily broken."

Maybe you understand that all too well, and you long desperately to have that companion these verses are talking about. In your desire and haste for companionship, you must be careful to heed the *Holy Bible*'s warning regarding the character and type of companion we should seek, lest we end up with grief and pain as our companion.

2 Timothy 2:22 tells us, "Run from anything that stimulates youthful lusts. Instead, pursue righteous living, faithfulness, love, and peace. Enjoy the companionship of those who call on the Lord with pure hearts."

If this is the type of companion you seek, take it to the Lord in prayer. Ask Him to guide you in revealing the true character of each person you meet.

*Dear Heavenly Father,*

*We long for companionship that is pure and true, with a heart longing after You.*

*Test our hearts and prove that our motivation is right, Father. We thank You for serving as the perfect example of companionship through the person of Your son, Jesus Christ.*

*Help us to be a pure and true companion to others. Keep our hearts honest and right before You, Father. Give us wisdom, understanding and discernment always in choosing companionship.*

*Lead us in Your pathway of truth, and protect us from any and all evil influences, Father.*

*Father, protect us, and may no evil thing be allowed to enter our heart, body, mind, spirit, or emotions. Bring into our lives the companion or companions of Your choosing.*

*We ask these things in Your perfect, holy name.*
*AMEN.*

# A Prayer for Purpose

God created each and every one of us for a very special purpose. Proverbs 16:4 tells us, "The Lord has made everything for his own purposes, even the wicked for a day of disaster."

He has a plan for your life.

But that doesn't mean that we can or should go about living our lives without any thought because God is our great puppet master in the heavens. No, the *Holy Bible* clearly tells us in John 10:10, "The thief's purpose is to steal and kill and destroy. My purpose is to give them a rich and satisfying life."

We are in the midst of a spiritual battle. God longs to give us victory over sin and death, but there is a thief among us—a wolf. Many times, he dresses in sheep's clothing—the better to see, hear and taste us.

God's purpose is that none of us should perish, but that all should come to know Him. We are all a part of this divine plan, and God longs for us to be unified in this purpose for His glory. Romans 8:28 says, "And we know that God causes everything to work together for the good of those who love God and are called according to his purpose for them."

If we are unified in our purpose of bringing glory and honor to God, then we must set about using the abilities and talents He has given us for His glory—not our own.

I Corinthians 9:26 says, "So I run with purpose in every step. I am not just shadowboxing."

C. S. Lewis once said, "Aim at heaven and you will get earth thrown in. Aim at earth and you get neither."

Ask God to fulfill His purpose in your life today.

*Dear Heavenly Father,*

*We cry out to You, asking and believing that You will fulfill Your purpose in and for our lives (Psalm 57:2). Thank You for Your awesome power at work in our lives. We praise You for all of creation, and that not even the smallest detail of Your creation will disappear until its purpose is achieved (Matthew 5:18).*

*Father, we ask that You lead us and guide us as we read Your Word, showing us the unique talents and abilities, You are calling us to use for the glory and honor of Your purpose.*

*Protect us from temptation, Father. Guard our bodies, hearts, minds, spirits, and emotions from any and all evil.*

*May we run with endurance the race You have set before us (Hebrews 12:1). And, may we run in such a way as to win the prize (I Corinthians 9:24), that You may say to us, "Well done, my good and faithful servant (Matthew 25:21)."*

*Forgive us for selfish ambitions and following after worldly lusts that don't satisfy us.*

*We thank You, Father, that one day we will celebrate the accomplishment of Your purpose together in Heaven.*

*In Your precious, holy name we pray.*
*AMEN.*

# A Prayer for Effective Use of Time

Something that is equal to all of us is the amount of time available for us each day we live. How we choose to use the time we are given is what makes the difference in each of our lives. Often, we would like time to stand still in our lives, while at other times we wish to fast forward. In either case, how is it that we can most effectively use the time God has given to each of us?

Ecclesiastes reminds us that there is a time for every purpose under heaven. We know that we were created for God's purposes. Knowing this, we must be careful to make the most of the limited time God has given to us. Ephesians 5:15-17 tells us, "So be careful how you live. Don't live like fools, but like those who are wise. Make the most of every opportunity in these evil days. Don't act thoughtlessly but understand what the Lord wants you to do."

Effective use of time means that we act in such a way as to make the most of our Master's assets—the talents He has given to us—as illustrated in the Parable of the Three Servants, recorded in Matthew 25:14-30.

"Again, the Kingdom of Heaven can be illustrated by the story of a man going on a long trip. He called together his servants and entrusted his money to them while he was gone. He gave five bags of silver to one, two bags of silver to another, and one bag of silver to the last—dividing it in proportion to their abilities. He then left on his trip. The servant who received the five bags of silver began to invest the money and earned five more. The servant with two bags of silver also went to work and earned two more. But the servant who received the one bag of silver dug a hole in the ground and hid the master's money. After a long time their master returned from his trip and called them to give an account of how they had used his money. The servant to whom he had entrusted the five bags of silver came forward with five more and said, 'Master, you gave me five bags of silver to invest, and I have earned five more.' The master was full of praise. 'Well done, my good and faithful servant. You have been faithful in handling this small amount, so now I will give you many more responsibilities. Let's celebrate together!' The servant who had received the two bags of silver came forward and said, 'Master, you gave me two bags of silver to invest, and I have earned two more.' The master said, 'Well done, my good and faithful servant. You have been faithful in handling this small amount, so now I will give you many more responsibilities. Let's celebrate together!' Then the servant with the one bag of silver came and said, 'Master, I knew you were a harsh man, harvesting crops you didn't plant and gathering crops you didn't cultivate. I was afraid I would lose your money, so I hid it in the earth. Look, here is your money back.' But the master replied, 'You wicked and lazy servant! If you knew I harvested crops I didn't plant and gathered crops I didn't cultivate, why didn't you deposit my money in the bank? At least I could have gotten some interest on it.' Then he ordered, 'Take the money from this servant, and give it to the one with the ten bags of silver. To those who use well what they are given, even more will be given, and they will have an abundance. But from those who do nothing, even what little they have will be taken away. Now throw this useless servant into outer darkness, where there will be weeping and gnashing of teeth.'"

We all want to hear God say, "Well done, my good and faithful servant." But, in order to hear that, we must be doers of His Word and not hearers only (James 1:22).

*Dear Heavenly Father,*

*Remind me of how brief my life on earth will be. Remind me that my days are numbered and how fleeting my life is (Psalm 39:4).*

*Grant us effective use of every moment we breathe. We thank You, Father, for the many gifts and talents You have given to us. May we use them always for Your glory—not our own.*

*We praise You for the opportunity to be a blessing to others. Help us to be mindful of the needs of others. May we follow Your example of humility and service in all our hands find to do.*

*Guide us in making the most of all times, including times of adversity. May we learn and grow in wisdom and understanding Father— deliberate and careful about every choice we make.*

*We ask all these things in Your precious, holy name.*
*AMEN.*

# A Prayer in Time of Public Disgrace

Are you in the midst of some great, publicly exposed deception? Do you feel disgraced as a result of your own act or acts of deception? Or, perhaps you have fallen victim to the betrayal of another—leading to a very public exposé of sin. We can all think of someone who has experienced such a public disgrace, but now it is you. You are experiencing the disgrace.

Proverbs 11:2 says, "Pride leads to disgrace, but with humility comes wisdom."

There is a wonderful promise regarding disgrace in Psalm 25:3, "No one who trusts in you will ever be disgraced, but disgrace comes to those who try to deceive others."

If you have been obedient to God and trust in Him, He promises that you will never be disgraced. That is an amazing promise.

However, if you are the one who has deceived, there is a penalty, a consequence for your sin. It is a comfort to know that God does not punish His children forever. When we take the time to repent, to turn from our sin, God receives us with open arms and restores us into His loving favor once again.

As Isaiah 57:15 tells us, "The high and lofty one who lives in eternity, the Holy One, says this: 'I live in the high and holy place with those whose spirits are contrite and humble. I restore the crushed spirit of the humble and revive the courage of those with repentant hearts.'"

God loves us so much, caring even the way we are received and perceived by others. May we look to Him as our deliverer in all things.

"Those who look to him for help will be radiant with joy; no shadow of shame will darken their faces" (Psalm 34:5).

*Dear Heavenly Father,*

*We thank You that You have the power to remove our shame and disgrace. Lord, help us to focus on Your perception of us, rather than the perception of others.*

*You know our hearts, Father, and we ask that You vindicate us in charges that are false against us. We also ask that You forgive us and cleanse our hearts from the wrong we have done.*

*Father, deliver us from the temptation to do evil. Enable us to forgive others for their public flogging of us.*

*Do a magnificent work in our hearts and lives that would bring glory and honor to Your name only.*

*Enable us to make right any and all wrong we have committed.*

*It is in Your precious, holy name we pray.*

*AMEN.*

# A Prayer to Be Understood

Do you ever feel as though others view you to be an alien from an unknown planet? Do you wish that someone could look into your soul and understand who you are, what you think, and the planet that you've come from? If you're answer is, "yes," to any of these questions, you're not alone. Countless other people have felt just as you do—including Jesus.

However, the key to filling this need or desire in your life is not found in selfishly longing to be understood. The key is found in pursuing a deeper understanding of the One who created us—the One true and living God.

Jeremiah 4:22 says, "My people are foolish and do not know me," says the Lord. "They are stupid children who have no understanding. They are clever enough at doing wrong, but they have no idea how to do right!"

Ouch! But, so true of us so very often, isn't it? We are so busy being absorbed in our own sinful idiosyncrasies, longing for someone to find us *special* that we lose sight of the One who truly made us *special*—the only One who truly understands us better than anyone on earth ever will.

*Dear Heavenly Father,*

*I feel so very alone and long to be understood, but I know that Your grace and Your goodness are sufficient to meet that longing in my life.*

*Father, I want to understand You. Help me understand the meaning of Your commandments, and I will meditate on your wonderful deeds (Psalm 119:27).*

*Thank You for understanding me, Lord. Thank You for creating me in Your image (Genesis 1:27). Forgive me for my selfishness, Father. Draw me ever near You and keep me from any and all evil temptations.*

*May my life reflect an understanding of Your ways, that You may fulfill my desire to be understood.*

*In Your precious, holy name I pray.*
*AMEN.*

# A Prayer for Someone to Listen

In Job 31:35, Job cries out, "If only someone would listen to me!"

Do you share Job's sentiment? Do you feel alone, and though no one will listen to you?

In Job's story, there were three close friends of his whom, upon hearing of his tragedy, came to comfort and console him. They sat with him for seven days and nights without saying a word since they saw that his suffering was too great for words.

Yet, when Job finally spoke after the seven days, his friends did not listen. Each one, in turn, had Job's plight entirely figured out. They continued to speak, rambling on and on, pouring salt in each and every one of Job's many wounds.

Not only did Job's friends not listen to what he had to say, they accused him of being arrogant, faithless, disobedient, and guilty of all manner of hidden sins! Certainly, with friends like Job had, he didn't need enemies.

In desperation for someone to listen, Job cried out to God, criticizing Him and assuming He would not listen, either. But God did listen. God did respond. He lovingly and firmly reminded Job of his place in the world.

Then, God blessed Job beyond anything he could ever hope or imagine.

God can and will listen to you, too, and He has the ability to bless you beyond anything you could ever hope or imagine.

*Dear Heavenly Father,*

*We thank You that Your Word reminds us that You bend down and listen to us. Because You listen, we will pray as long as we have breath, Father (Psalm 116:2).*

*Thank You, Lord, for being always with us to comfort us in our loneliness and to listen to each and every thought that enters our mind. You are so great, Father. We are totally and completely amazed that You are even mindful of us at all, for we are but a vapor.*

*Father, help us to listen to others. Help us to hear them when they truly need to be heard. Help us to take up the cause of the weak and wounded, Father, as You take up our every concern and cause.*

*Please forgive us for our arrogance in days past. We come humbly to You, Father, thanking You for the gift of life. May we use each breath that You give us for Your glory and Your honor, Father.*

*Lord, You know we groan within our solitude. Please grant relief, and through our groaning, may we learn what You desire for us to learn.*

*For it is in Your precious, holy name we pray.*
*AMEN.*

# A Prayer for Kindness

The world can be a cold, cruel and lonely place. For many reasons, kindness can often be very hard to find. Proverbs 19:22 says, "What is desired in a man is kindness, and a poor man is better than a liar."

Ruth knew all too well that the world could be a very cruel and lonely place. Her husband died, and she moved to another land with her mother-in-law, Naomi, where she knew no one. Naomi was also a widow, and the two women were alone as they traveled back to Naomi's homeland.

Yet, it wasn't long before the two women were overwhelmed with kindness. A man named Boaz, a relative of Naomi's, had allowed Ruth to glean grain in his fields along with his workers. Boaz also protected Ruth and provided food and water to her while she worked in his field. Ruth and Naomi were both very grateful for his kindness.

In Ruth 2:10-11 we read, "Ruth fell at his feet and thanked him warmly. "What have I done to deserve such kindness?" she asked. "I am only a foreigner."

"Yes, I know," Boaz replied. "But I also know about everything you have done for your mother-in-law since the death of your husband. I have heard how you left your father and mother and your own land to live here among complete strangers."

Ruth was reaping the kindness she had sown in the life of her mother-in-law, Naomi. The *Holy Bible* reminds us in Galatians 6:7, "Don't be misled—you cannot mock the justice of God. You will always harvest what you plant."

Are you, like Ruth, planting a crop of kindness in the lives of others? If so, you will surely reap what you have planted.

*Dear Heavenly Father,*

*Thank You for Your infinite loving kindness for us. Help us to plant a crop of kindness in the lives of everyone we meet and everyone we know.*

*Father, we are in need of kindness. Please help us to find kindness in this world. We know and believe that kindness exists. And, when we find it, help us to give back sevenfold for the kindness we have received.*

*Remind us always of Your kindness, Lord.*

*May we never let loyalty and kindness leave us (Proverbs 3:3). We thank You that Your Word promises that our kindness will reward us (Proverbs 11:17).*

*Forgive us for any cruelty we have exhibited, Father, and help us to be kind to others always.*

*We praise You and thank You for showing us Your ways.*

*In Your perfect, holy name we pray.*

*AMEN.*

# A Prayer for Times of Rejection

"He was despised and rejected—a man of sorrows, acquainted with deepest grief. We turned our backs on him and looked the other way. He was despised, and we did not care" (Isaiah 53:3).

That man was Jesus. He has been right where you are today. He faced rejection not once, but repeatedly. John 1:11 tells us, "He came to his own people, and even they rejected him."

Perhaps that is the case with you today. Everyone has turned against you. Even your own family has rejected you.

The *Holy Bible* tells us in Matthew 21:42, "Then Jesus asked them, 'Didn't you ever read this in the Scriptures? The stone that the builders rejected has now become the cornerstone. This is the Lord's doing, and it is wonderful to see.'"

Jesus knew and believed that He would receive His acceptance and reward for doing the will of the Father.

Are you doing the will of Your Heavenly Father? If you are, then you can be sure that God is taking up your cause.

There is a beautiful passage of Scripture relating to salvation of the Israelites that is applicable to you today. It is Romans 11:15, "For since their rejection meant that God offered salvation to the rest of the world, their acceptance will be even more wonderful. It will be life for those who were dead!"

When Christ accepts you, there is no need for acceptance from anyone else in the rest of the world. Christ is enough. He is all you need.

*Dear Heavenly Father,*

*Thank You for accepting me. I praise You and thank You because I know You are all that I need.*

*My heart is overwhelmed and hurting from all the rejection I have faced and continue to face in every direction. Please still my anxious heart and anxious thoughts. Help me to feel Your acceptance. Send Your comforting Holy Spirit to surround me, Father, reminding me that You accept me when I do what is right (Genesis 4:7). Help me to be strong and not allow sin to control me.*

*Lord, help me not to reject others as I have been rejected—but only to reject sin. May I be accepting and loving of others as a part of Your grand creation.*

*Forgive me for my many failings, Father. Strengthen me when my faith is weak.*

*Father, I thank You and praise You for bearing my rejection on the cross. Help me to serve You all the days of my life.*

*In Your precious, holy name I pray.*
*AMEN.*

# A Prayer for a Godly Mate

Randy Pausch, author of *The Last Lecture*, was asked by Oprah Winfrey what advice he would give to his daughter in consideration of selecting a future mate. His response was that his daughter should pay no attention to what a potential mate may say, but she should pay attention to what he does.

In a marriage, as in any relationship, our actions speak so much louder than our words. Our actions indicate our true character—our substance.

I don't know where you are today. You may be single and looking for a mate. You may be widowed. Or, you may be married, and desiring your mate to have a heart for the things of God. Wherever you find yourself, believe that God can and will help you. Tell Him all that is on Your heart.

The *Holy Bible* provides us with a wonderful example of the type of mate we should seek. We should seek to be married to a Christian, as 2 Corinthians 6:14 says, "Don't team up with those who are unbelievers. How can righteousness be a partner with wickedness? How can light live with darkness?"

Be sure to examine the actions of your potential mate, assuring that their walk matches their talk. And, never neglect to bring your concerns before Your Heavenly Father. He cares about even the smallest details of Your significant life.

*Dear Heavenly Father,*

*Thank You for caring about every detail of my life. It is my desire to have a Godly mate. Please make that possible for me, Lord, and if that is not Your plan for my life, then I ask that You take away that desire.*

*Help me to be the kind of person that others see as Godly. I praise You for bringing me to this difficult place in order that You may teach me more of Your way, and fashion me in accordance with Your will for my life.*

*Father, I thank You that Your Word promises that You are my husband and redeemer (Isaiah 54:5).*

*May Your love and companionship sustain me at all times.*

*In Your perfect, holy name I pray.*

*AMEN.*

# A Prayer for True Friendship

*"Many will say they are loyal friends, but who can find one who is truly reliable"* (Proverbs 20:6)?

The *Holy Bible* paints a beautiful picture of true friendship through the story of David and Jonathan. 1 Samuel 18:1 tells us, "After David had finished talking with Saul, he met Jonathan, the king's son. There was an immediate bond between them, for Jonathan loved David."

The passage goes on to say in 1 Samuel 18:3-4, "And Jonathan made a solemn pact with David, because he loved him as he loved himself. Jonathan sealed the pact by taking off his robe and giving it to David, together with his tunic, sword, bow, and belt."

This was a very dangerous commitment for Jonathan, since King Saul despised David, the newly anointed but not yet appointed King. Jonathan's friendship was active. He proved his love for David in every circumstance. Saul tried to murder David numerous times. Yet, Jonathan took up David's cause against his father—risking his own life.

The *Holy Bible* tells us that, "There is no greater love than to lay down one's life for one's friends" (John 15:13).

The *Holy Bible* also tells us in Proverbs 18:24, "There are 'friends' who destroy each other, but a real friend sticks closer than a brother."

I know a friend like that. He is a friend of sinners (Matthew 11:19). Psalm 25:14 says, "The Lord is a friend to those who fear him. He teaches them his covenant."

Just imagine it—friendship with the Lord. There is no truer friendship than His.

*Dear Heavenly Father,*

*Thank You for being a friend to those who fear You. Help me to fear You, Father. I long to have a true friend. Thank You that You are the truest of friends who ever was or ever will be.*

*Keep me close to You, dear Father. May I never place anyone or anything before You. May the seeds of my good deeds become a tree of life and win friends (Proverbs 11:30).*

*Lord, help me to be the kind of friend who sticks closer than a brother (Proverbs 18:24). Purify my heart and bless me with gracious speech that I may have the king as my friend (Proverbs 22:11).*

*Give me the ability to accept the heartfelt counsel of friends for what it is—as sweet as perfume and incense (Proverbs 27:9).*

*Most of all, Father, may I be always obedient to Your call upon my life in every circumstance.*

*In Your precious name I pray.*
*AMEN.*

# SECTION IX

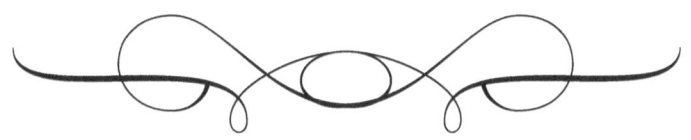

rayers

*for* TIMES *of* FEAR

# A Prayer for Protection

"The Lord is my rock, my fortress, and my savior; my God is my rock, in whom I find protection. He is my shield, the power that saves me, and my place of safety" (Psalm 18:2).

God's divine protection is evident in countless miracles occurring every second of every day. My favorite *Holy Bible* story evidencing this truth is the story of Daniel in the lion's den.

In the story, the counselors and administrators in King Darius' court persuaded him to sign a decree making it a crime to pray to anyone other than King Darius. Any violator of this law was to be thrown into the den of lions.

Upon learning of this new decree, Daniel went home to his upstairs room and knelt before an open window to pray. Daniel's customary practice was to kneel and pray, giving thanks to God three times each day.

When the officials in King Darius' court found Daniel praying to God, they informed the King, reminding him of the decree. The situation disturbed King Darius greatly because he thought very highly of Daniel. King Darius spent the rest of the day trying to think of a way to rescue Daniel from his own decree. Daniel 6:15-16 tell us what happened next, "In the evening the men went together to the king and said, 'Your Majesty, you know that according to the law of the Medes and the Persians, no law that the king signs can be changed.' So at last the king gave orders for Daniel to be arrested and thrown into the den of lions. The king said to him, "May your God, whom you serve so faithfully, rescue you."

When Daniel was thrown into the lion's den, a stone was rolled in front to seal the opening—preventing anyone from rescuing Daniel. The king couldn't sleep all night, and when he returned to the lion's den the next morning, he found Daniel without a scratch on him! The King then ordered Daniel's accusers and their families to be thrown into the lion's den. The *Holy Bible* tells us that the lions leaped on them and tore them apart before they even hit the floor.

Psalm 31:19 says, "How great is the goodness you have stored up for those who fear you. You lavish it on those who come to you for protection, blessing them before the watching world."

*Dear Heavenly Father,*

*We thank You and praise You for protection from evil. We praise You that Your Word tells us that the fear of the Lord leads to life, bringing security and protection from harm (Proverbs 19:23).*

*Father, we trust in You for protection (Psalm 11:1). We thank You for being a shield to all who come to You for protection (Proverbs 30:5).*

*We thank You, Heavenly Father, that You are like a wide river of protection that no enemy can cross, that no enemy ship can sail upon (Isaiah 33:21).*

*Help us in times of fear and doubt.*

*May we always depend upon You, Father, for we know that You will never fail us. You have never failed us. We praise You for who You are, Lord.*

*Guard our bodies, minds, hearts, souls, spirits and emotions from any and all evil that may seek to destroy us.*

*Thank You for Your constant protection in and around us.*

*In Your precious, holy name we pray.*

*AMEN.*

# A Prayer for Removal of Danger

"For we are not fighting against flesh-and-blood enemies, but against evil rulers and authorities of the unseen world, against mighty powers in this dark world, and against evil spirits in the heavenly places" (Ephesians 6:12).

The *Holy Bible* tells us that many of the dangers that we face are unseen. If these dangers cannot be seen with the natural eye, then how do we recognize them and combat them? How do we remove them?

Ephesians 6:13-17 reminds us to put on the whole armor of God. It says, "Therefore, put on every piece of God's armor so you will be able to resist the enemy in the time of evil. Then after the battle you will still be standing firm. Stand your ground, putting on the belt of truth and the body armor of God's righteousness. For shoes, put on the peace that comes from the Good News so that you will be fully prepared. In addition to all of these, hold up the shield of faith to stop the fiery arrows of the devil. Put on salvation as your helmet, and take the sword of the Spirit, which is the word of God."

This passage of Scripture goes on to tell us to pray at all times and on every occasion, to stay alert and to be persistent in our prayers!

In Luke 8, Jesus was sleeping in a boat when the disciples woke Him to explain the great danger they were facing. A storm had arisen, and they were in danger of drowning. Jesus rebuked them for their lack of faith and commanded the wind and waves to be still—removing the imminent danger they were facing.

Romans 8:35 reminds us that there is nothing, no danger that can separate us from the love of God. Pray, obediently seek God, and have faith that He will remove the dangers you are facing today.

*Dear Heavenly Father,*

*We thank You for being able to conquer and remove any danger we are facing in our lives today, whether seen or unseen. We ask You to intervene in our lives today and remove the danger of _____ from our lives today.*

*We praise You for the many times You have gone before us and removed dangers that we have not seen. Thank You, Father, for growing our faith and drawing our hearts to You through times of danger.*

*Lord, today we put on Your full armor. We put on the belt of truth, the body armor of Your righteousness, the shoes of peace, the helmet of salvation, the sword of the Spirit, and we hold up the shield of faith to stop the fiery arrows of the devil.*

*Thank You for equipping us with these tools to combat and remove danger from our lives. Give us prudence, Father, and wisdom. We ask that we may have a discerning Spirit to know when and how to act in any and every situation we face.*

*Thank You for casting out our fears through Your perfect love (I John 4:18).*
*In Your precious name we pray.*
*AMEN.*

# A Prayer for a Hiding Place

*"For you are my hiding place; you protect me from trouble. You surround me with songs of victory"* (Psalm 32:7).

The Book of Psalms is filled with verses regarding God as our hiding place.

David was a man after God's own heart (Acts 13:22). He was not a perfect man, but he followed obediently after God for the greater part of his life. In spite of David's obedience to God and desire to please Him, David still encountered a number of trials, temptations and difficulties. David was attacked by King Saul, his best friend's father, who tried numerous times to kill him. Yet, in each attempt on David's life, God provided a hiding place for him.

David faced angry mobs of people and attempts on his life. Even King David's own son, Absalom, rebelled against him in an attempt to take the kingdom away from his father. And, at each sign of trouble, God again provided a hiding place for David.

In Joshua 2, we learn how God provided a hiding place for two spies Joshua sent into Jericho as the Israelites were planning to take possession of the land God had promised them. Rahab, a woman who had previously made her living through prostitution, was used by God to provide a hiding place for the two men.

There is no trouble so great that God cannot provide a hiding place for you. Psalm 27:5 says, "For he will conceal me there when troubles come; he will hide me in his sanctuary. He will place me out of reach on a high rock."

*Dear Heavenly Father,*

*Thank You for being my hiding place. I come to You when I am afraid, and You surround me with Your tender mercies so I may live (Psalm 119:77).*

*I praise You, Father, that You are my sanctuary—a safe place I can run to and find a place to hide. You calm my fears, Father.*

*Keep my heart focused and obedient to Your Word, Father. Guard me safely in Your embrace, Father.*

*Lord, when I am afraid, I will trust in You (Psalm 56:3). Help my times of doubt and unbelief.*

*And, Father, when it is within my ability to do so, help me to be a hiding place for others who are in need of shelter.*

*In Your precious, holy name we pray.*
*AMEN.*

# A Prayer for Safe Passage

Zechariah 10:11-12 paints a beautiful picture of God's provision for safe passage to His people. "They will pass safely through the sea of distress, for the waves of the sea will be held back, and the waters of the Nile will dry up. The pride of Assyria will be crushed, and the rule of Egypt will end. By my power I will make my people strong, and by my authority they will go wherever they wish. I, the Lord, have spoken!"

Think of it. There you are facing an insurmountable obstacle. Just like in the preschool game, *Goin' on a Bear Hunt*, you can't go over it, under it, or around it. You have to go through it. But you don't have to go through it alone.

Psalm 23:4 says, "Even when I walk through the darkest valley, I will not be afraid, for you are close beside me."

Acts 23 tells of a conspiracy by over forty men to kill the apostle Paul. The religious leaders charged Paul with violating the religious law of the Jews. Paul's enemies planned to have the high council ask the commander to bring Paul back to the council under the pretense of examining his case more closely.

God provided a way of safe passage for Paul. His nephew heard about the plot against Paul's life. When the commander learned of the plan, he sent two hundred troops to protect Paul and escort him safely to Governor Felix.

God can provide safe passage for you, too.

*Dear Heavenly Father,*

*Thank You for the many times You have blessed us with safe passage. We ask, once again, that You would grant us safe passage as we _____ .*

*Calm our fears, Father, and fill us with faith and trust in You. Lord, we know that You have a plan for the ultimate good of all who love You.*

*Help us to act swiftly, with the cunning of a serpent and the gentleness of a dove. We ask that You guard and protect us from the evil one and help us to hear Your voice as it calls to us, directing us to Your path of truth.*

*We praise You, Father, that we never have to walk alone, for You are always with us. Keep us close to You at all times, abiding in obedience, and forgive us for our sins against You and others.*

*We ask these things in Your precious, holy name.*
*AMEN.*

# A Prayer for Defense

Many frightening battles that we face require a defense—an advocate for our cause. What better defense could you possibly have than the Creator of the Universe? There is none.

The *Holy Bible* tells us in Psalm 34:7, "For the angel of the Lord is a guard; he surrounds and defends all who fear him."

In the story of David and Goliath, we find one of the most dramatic pictures of God's defense at work in the lives of His faithful. 1 Samuel 17 tells the story.

The Philistine army was camped across from the Israelites. Goliath was a Philistine giant, standing over nine feet tall. Day after day, Goliath taunted the Israelites, asking for one man to fight. If the man defeated Goliath, the Philistines would become the slaves of the Israelites; but, if Goliath defeated the man, the Israelites would become Philistine slaves.

Jesse, David's father, had been helping to tend sheep and run errands while his three oldest brothers were fighting against the Philistines. One day, Jesse sent David with some food for his brothers, and asked him to report back as to how they were doing. When David learned about Goliath, he told King Saul that he wanted to fight Goliath. David's brothers and the King scoffed at David, but he was undeterred. David said, "The LORD who rescued me from the claws of the lion and the bear will rescue me from this Philistine" (I Samuel 17:37)!

David gathered five smooth stones, placed them in his sling, and the God of the Universe enabled him to defeat Goliath, without spear or sword.

Do you have faith in God? If so, you have the greatest defender in the Universe on your side in defense of you today.

*Dear Heavenly Father,*

*We need You as an advocate today, Father. We need You to come to our defense regarding _____.*

*We thank You and praise You, Father, that Your Word tells us that wisdom is a defense, as money is a defense (Ecclesiastes 7:12). We thank You that these defenses come from You and You alone.*

*Father, we praise You for being the defender of the defenseless, orphans, widows, and all the things that the world views as "lost causes".*

*Lord, we thank You that we have victory in and through You alone. Help us to defend those in need of our help—in need of an advocate. May we always follow Your example in being a defender of what is true and right.*

*Forgive us for the many ways in which we have failed You. Draw us close to You so that we may be obedient to Your plan and purpose for our lives here on earth.*

*In Your precious, holy name we pray.*
*AMEN.*

# A Prayer for Awareness of Danger

"A prudent person foresees danger and takes precautions. The simpleton goes blindly on and suffers the consequences" (Proverbs 22:3).

Jochebed was the mother of Moses. At the time he was born, the Pharaoh issued a decree that all newborn baby boys should be thrown into the Nile River. Jochebed recognized that this baby boy was special. After hiding the baby for three months, she foresaw the impending death of her newborn baby and hid him in a basket made of papyrus reeds, placing him in the Nile River.

Moses was found by Pharaoh's daughter, who had great compassion for him. Jochebed acted on her awareness of danger, and Moses' life was spared.

In the story of Abigail, Nabal, and David in 1 Samuel 25, God blessed Abigail with an awareness of the danger awaiting her household as a result of her husband's foolish actions. David's men protected Nabal and all he owned, asking only for Nabal to share some of his provisions with them during the time of celebration and sheep shearing. But, Nabal sneered and mocked David and his men, denying their request for favor.

When Abigail learned what happened, she acted immediately by taking provisions to David and his men. As a result, Abigail and her household were spared.

It isn't enough to simply be aware of danger. Scripture tells us we must act by taking precautions.

Ask God to give you an awareness of danger and to act in accordance with His Word today.

*Dear Heavenly Father,*

*Thank You that You are omnipotent, omniscient, and omnipresent in our lives. We are struggling with fear, Father, and ask that You would give us an awareness of danger in and around us. Lord, we also ask that You give us wisdom and prudence in taking action once You have made us aware of such danger.*

*We thank You, Father, that You have not given us a spirit of fear and timidity, but of power, love and self-discipline (2 Timothy 1:7).*

*We praise You, Father, that there is nothing in all creation that can separate us from Your love for us.*

*Help us to be obedient to You, acting on faith in accordance with Your Word at all times. We worship You with holy fear and awe for giving us an unshakable Kingdom (Hebrews 12:28).*

*Forgive us when we doubt, Lord, and help our unbelief.*

*In Your holy name we pray.*

*AMEN.*

# A Prayer for a Sense of Reality

We have all met people whom we felt did not have a good sense of reality. Perhaps they had an unrealistic view of themselves or situations in the world around them. Or, maybe they had an unrealistic perception of others.

In our world of reality television programs on every channel, it seems as though more than ever before, people are searching for reality. Yet, true reality abides in the truth that comes from knowing and experiencing God.

Dr. Henry Blackaby's *Holy Bible* study entitled, *Experiencing God*, deals directly with our need for a reality check. Anything other than knowing and experiencing the one true and living God at work in and through our lives every day is not reality—it is not truth.

The *Holy Bible* tells us in Colossians 3:1-4, "Since you have been raised to new life with Christ, set your sights on the realities of heaven, where Christ sits in the place of honor at God's right hand. Think about the things of heaven, not the things of earth. For you died to this life, and your real life is hidden with Christ in God. And when Christ, who is your life, is revealed to the whole world, you will share in all his glory."

When we fill our lives with things other than Christ, we are merely using cheap substitutes to create a false sense of reality in our lives. We must turn to God in worship, praise, and thanksgiving to experience true reality. Through prayer, we can do all of these things.

Proverbs 27:19 says, "As a face is reflected in water, so the heart reflects the real person."

*Dear Heavenly Father,*

*We desire to really know you—to know and experience the reality that can come only through a close, personal relationship with You.*

*We thank You for providing truth and reality in our lives. Please purge any and all evil from our lives, Father. Fill us with Your truth and Your light.*

*Help us to gain a heart of wisdom so that we may avoid deception in every area of our lives. May we truly experience You, Father. Help us to be pure. Help us to purge our bodies and minds from evil. Guard and keep us from allowing filth or any unclean thing to enter our lives in any way.*

*Lord, we ask that You make us into a consistent lighthouse for You that would display reality to others.*

*We praise You for being real, Father.*

*It is in Your most holy and precious name we pray.*

*AMEN.*

# A Prayer for Protection by Angels

"For he will order his angels to protect you wherever you go" (Psalm 91:11).

The *Holy Bible* is full of stories in which God uses His angels to protect His people. Lot was aggressively protected by angels during the destruction of Sodom and Gomorrah as recorded in Genesis 19. The *Holy Bible* says that the angels told Lot to take his wife and family and get out of the city quickly or they would be swept away in the destruction of the city. Genesis 19:16 says, "When Lot still hesitated, the angels seized his hand and the hands of his wife and two daughters and rushed them to safety outside the city, for the Lord was merciful."

An angel of God called to Hagar—providing comfort and the promise of God's protection—when she was wandering in the wilderness with her son, Ishmael, after being sent away by Abraham and Sarah (Genesis 21:17).

The angel of the Lord stopped Abraham's hand from killing Isaac in Genesis 22:12.

In Exodus 23:20, God promised to send his angel of protection ahead of the Israelites into the land of the Amorites, Hittites, Perizzites, Canaanites, Hivites, and Jebusites, so the Israelites could live there and possess the land.

Angels also came to take care of Jesus after He was tempted by Satan in the wilderness (Matthew 4:11).

This is only the beginning of the numerous accounts of God using His angels to protect His chosen ones.

Hebrews 1:14 tell us, "Therefore, angels are only servants—spirits sent to care for people who will inherit salvation."

May God's angels protect and care for you in your time of need.

*Dear Heavenly Father,*

*We thank You and praise You for sending Your angels to protect and care for us in our many times of need. Please send your angels to guard and protect us today from _____.*

*Father, please comfort us and strengthen our faith in You. May Your angels surround us, imparting Your heavenly presence to us.*

*Keep us in obedience, Lord. Guard us from any and all evil. We thank You that You care so much for us that You send angels to minister around us.*

*We worship and praise You, Father, for drawing us unto You and providing constant protection from our fears.*

*Forgive us for doubting, Father.*

*Keep us in the center of Your plan and purpose for our lives.*

*We ask these things in Your precious, holy name.*

*AMEN.*

# A Prayer for the Protection of Others

In the 6th Chapter of Ephesians, Paul reminds us of the importance of staying in constant communion with God through prayer. Paul is in prison, and he is writing to the church at Ephesus to ask them to pray for him.

Has someone asked you to pray for them? Or, do you know of someone in need of protection?

Ephesians 6:18 says, "Pray in the Spirit at all times and on every occasion. Stay alert and be persistent in your prayers for all believers everywhere."

When we are aware of the needs of others and it is in our power to act on their behalf, the Word of God commands us to act. James 4:17 tells us, "Remember, it is sin to know what you ought to do and then not do it."

If we are aware of someone in need of prayer, it is our responsibility to pray for them. How much greater is our responsibility if we are aware that someone is in need of protection.

Proverbs 30:5 says, "Every word of God proves true. He is a shield to all who come to him for protection."

*Dear Heavenly Father,*

*Guard the life of _____ from _____. We ask that You would be a shield around them—a hedge of protection in this situation. Grant _____ wisdom and rest in the assurance of Your Word.*

*Father, please remove any and all evil from coming anywhere near _____.*

*Give them perceptive eyes and ears to the dangers around them. Help them to be loyal and obedient to You, for you guard and protect those who follow You, Father (Psalm 97:10).*

*We claim Your promise of protection for us, Lord.*

*Help us to trust, depend and rely solely on You for our protection, Father, and may we act prudently and in accordance with Your commands.*

*We ask all these things in Your name.*
*AMEN.*

# A Prayer for Removal of Jealousy

"Anger is cruel, and wrath is like a flood, but jealousy is even more dangerous" (Proverbs 27:4).

The *Holy Bible* speaks a great deal about the dangers of jealousy. It is a destructive force in our lives that often gives way to unrealistic anger and sin. Proverbs 14:30 says, "A peaceful heart leads to a healthy body; jealousy is like cancer in the bones."

Jealousy caused Joseph's brothers to throw him into a pit and sell him into slavery (Genesis 37). Jealousy caused Sarai to send Hagar packing (Genesis 16).

Jealousy also caused King Saul to attempt to murder David again and again and again (1 Samuel 18)!

Job 5:2 tells us that, "Surely resentment destroys the fool, and jealousy kills the simple."

James 3:15-16 tells us, "For jealousy and selfishness are not God's kind of wisdom. Such things are earthly, unspiritual, and demonic. For wherever there is jealousy and selfish ambition, there you will find disorder and evil of every kind."

God can purge this sin from your life if you will acknowledge it before Him and ask for His divine strength. We cannot cover it up or hide it, as James 3:14 tells us, "But if you are bitterly jealous and there is selfish ambition in your heart, don't cover up the truth with boasting and lying." When we confess our sin, Christ is faithful and just to forgive us and purify us from all unrighteousness (1 John 1:9).

Our God is a jealous God. He demands a total commitment from us. When we are totally committed to Him, it shows. Our lives bear much good fruit! We don't have to be jealous, nor must we be jealousy's object. Proverbs 12:12 says, "Thieves are jealous of each other's loot, but the godly are well rooted and bear their own fruit."

*Dear Heavenly Father,*

*Guard our lives from jealousy. Please purge this sin from affecting our lives in any way. Help us to commit totally and completely in obedience to You, Lord. Keep us in the center of Your will where there is no need and no lack of any good thing.*

*We thank You and praise You for Your love. We thank You that love is patient and kind, not jealous or boastful or proud (1 Corinthians 13:4).*

*Fill us with You, Father, and remove all unrealistic fear, causing jealousy in our lives. Remind us of our dependence on You as our source for all things.*

*Keep selfish ambition far from us, Father. In humility, we bring our weak and wounded lives before You in complete service and devotion. Pour us out and fill us totally and completely with You so that there is no room for jealousy or any evil thing, Father.*

*May we cease to be the object of jealousy, and may we never be the perpetrator of a jealous heart.*

*It is in Your most precious, holy name we pray, Father.*
*AMEN.*

# SECTION X

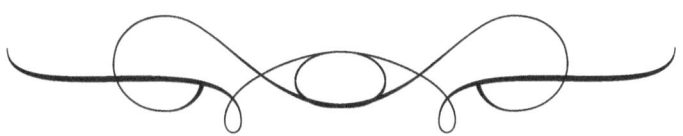

for TIMES of
WEAKNESS

# A Prayer for Strength

"And He said to me, 'My grace is sufficient for you, for My strength is made perfect in weakness.' Therefore most gladly I will rather boast in my infirmities, that the power of Christ may rest upon me" (2 Corinthians 12:9).

I don't know what crisis, what weakness has brought you to this page. But I do know that the Holy Spirit helps us in time of weakness. In fact, the *Holy Bible* tells us that the Holy Spirit helps us in knowing how to pray in our times of weakness.

Romans 8:26 tells us, "And the Holy Spirit helps us in our weakness. For example, we don't know what God wants us to pray for. But the Holy Spirit prays for us with groanings that cannot be expressed in words."

What God desires from us is total and complete dependence upon Him in faith. Then, we are useful to Him, and then we are in a place to receive His strength and blessing in our lives.

Isaiah 40:31 says, "But those who trust in the Lord will find new strength. They will soar high on wings like eagles. They will run and not grow weary. They will walk and not faint."

*Dear Heavenly Father,*

*We need Your strength. We know that Your power is made perfect in our weakness (2 Corinthians 12:9). Helps us to depend upon You, Father, and teach us how we should pray at this time.*

*Father, we are nothing without You. Restore our strength as we wait and depend upon You. We thank You that Your weakness is stronger than the greatest of human strength (1 Corinthians 1:25). Make us like You, Lord.*

*Forgive us for trying to do things in our own strength. Give us utterance in the things we should ask of You, Father.*

*We thank You and praise You for being our strength and our song, and for giving us victory through Your Holy Spirit.*

*We pray all these things in Your perfect, holy name.*
*AMEN.*

# A Prayer for Spiritual Growth

The apostle Paul prayed fervently for the spiritual growth of the church at Ephesus, as he writes in the Ephesians 3:14-21. Paul is encouraging the members of the church to come boldly before God's throne in prayer, prodding them to become excited about the glorious plan God has in revealing Himself to the Church.

Listen to Paul's heart as he prays for the Ephesians, "When I think of all this, I fall to my knees and pray to the Father, the Creator of everything in heaven and on earth. I pray that from his glorious, unlimited resources he will empower you with inner strength through his Spirit. Then Christ will make his home in your hearts as you trust in him. Your roots will grow down into God's love and keep you strong. And may you have the power to understand, as all God's people should, how wide, how long, how high, and how deep his love is. May you experience the love of Christ, though it is too great to understand fully. Then you will be made complete with all the fullness of life and power that comes from God."

"Now all glory to God, who is able, through his mighty power at work within us, to accomplish infinitely more than we might ask or think. Glory to him in the church and in Christ Jesus through all generations forever and ever! Amen."

Are you in need of spiritual growth in your life? I believe we are all in need of the growth Paul prays for in this passage.

Hebrews 5:11 warns us against spiritual dullness, and not listening to the truth. May God soften our hearts to be receptive to His truth and His call to action.

*Dear Heavenly Father,*

*How we long to grow closer to You! Draw us near, no matter what it takes to do so, Father. For we know that in You we find the fullness of every good thing! Help us to move beyond being babies into mature Christians who produce much good fruit in the lives of others by the power of Your name.*

*Forgive us, Lord, for making idols of other things in our lives. Help us to re-align our priorities with a focus on our relationship with You as most important.*

*We thank You and praise You for loving us so much that You draw us unto Yourself, Father. You are awesome, Lord. You are the fullness of joy, Father!*

*May we continue in passion to run the race of life, Lord. We want to be the winner—the one who hears You say, "Well done, my good and faithful servant (Matthew 25:21)!"*

*Help us to finish strong, Father, for it is in Your most holy name we pray.*
*AMEN.*

# A Prayer for Dependence on Christ

When I was a little girl growing up, my father told me often that I had quite an independent streak. He lovingly reminded me that this quality could prove to be either good or bad, depending upon the manner in which it was tempered.

Over time and on various occasions, my father found opportunities to remind me that God's ways were not our ways—that His thoughts were not our thoughts. In short, I was to have a servant's heart and follow the example of Christ in finding complete dependence upon God. I would listen and take every word to heart.

Yet, time and again, gradually my selfish and sinful independent nature would rear its ugly head—as if to remind God that I knew exactly how to respond to a given situation. Each time I acted on my own in this way, I was defeated.

Proverbs 3:5 says, "Trust in the Lord with all your heart; do not depend on your own understanding."

Lamentations 3:25 tells us, "The Lord is good to those who depend on him, to those who search for him."

Hosea 12:6 says, "So now, come back to your God. Act with love and justice, and always depend on him."

And, Matthew 19:14 tells us, "But Jesus said, 'Let the children come to me. Don't stop them! For the Kingdom of Heaven belongs to those who are like these children.'"

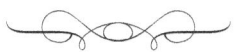

*Dear Heavenly Father,*

Forgive me for acting independent of You. I know that I can do all things through Christ who strengthens me (Philippians 4:13). I also know that apart from You I can do nothing (John 15:5).

Help me to depend upon You totally and completely in faith, Father, for You have never failed me. I know You will never fail me and praise You for that.

I praise You for loving me enough to teach me to be dependent upon You. I thank You for drawing me to You, Lord. Keep me always abiding in You, the true vine.

Lord, I praise You and thank You for meeting every need I have ever had in abundance. Forgive me for my lack of gratitude.

Thank You for being my living water, Father.

It is in Your precious, holy name I pray.

AMEN.

# A Prayer in Time of Marital Crisis

There is no limit to the variety of circumstances capable of causing marital crisis today. Yet, in each situation, God can hear your call for help, and He can direct the path that You should take.

Every situation is different. God sees them all. He sees each heart and knows what lies deep within. May I encourage you today to seek counsel in God's Word? In it we find truth to help in all times of need.

God's Word commands us to give honor to marriage. As Hebrews 13:4 tells us, "Give honor to marriage, and remain faithful to one another in marriage. God will surely judge people who are immoral and those who commit adultery."

As surely as God changed the heart of the Pharaoh to harden it in Exodus 4:21, He has the power to soften a heart—if it is part of His plan.

Our relationship with our spouse can also directly impact our worship. Malachi 2:14 says, "You cry out, 'Why doesn't the Lord accept my worship?' I'll tell you why! Because the Lord witnessed the vows you and your wife made when you were young. But you have been unfaithful to her, though she remained your faithful partner, the wife of your marriage vows."

My prayer for you today is that God would purify your heart, and nothing would hinder your prayers to the Father regarding your marriage.

*Dear Father in Heaven,*

*Our marriage needs help. Help us, Lord, to follow in Your ways. Remove all selfishness and sin from between us.*

*Father, heal our hurts. Help us to forgive each other and move forward in unified devotion to You, Lord.*

*Help us to guard our minds from any and all evil. May You take control of our tongues and help us not to wound each other with our words.*

*Help us to learn to trust each other again, but most of all, help us to trust completely in You together.*

*Thank You for making marriage, Lord. Thank You for my spouse, and all You are teaching me through this marriage.*

*In Your precious, holy name I pray.*
*AMEN.*

# A Prayer of Repentance

"If a person does not repent, God will sharpen his sword; he will bend and string his bow" (Psalm 7:12).

Repentance of sin is at the very foundation of our relationship with Christ. Without repentance, we are separated from God. Repentance is an acknowledgement of sin and a choice to turn away from sin—to choose, with God's strength, not to practice sin any longer. Repentance does not mean that we will be perfect, but rather that we are not accepting of our own sinful behavior. We are acknowledging that our sin is wrong.

When the people of Nineveh repented of their sins at the preaching of Jonah, God restored them to a position of favor and healed their land. He will heal and restore you, too.

The *Holy Bible* tells us that once we have repented of our sin, we must prove our repentance through our actions. Matthew 3:8 says, "Prove by the way you live that you have repented of your sins and turned to God."

When we have genuinely repented, it is evident to all. There is a change in us. There is a change in our want to. We no longer want to sin.

In Luke 5:32, Jesus says, "I have come to call not those who think they are righteous, but those who know they are sinners and need to repent."

*Dear Heavenly Father,*

*I am a sinner. I repent of my sin. Forgive me and change me, Father. I don't want to sin anymore. Help me to be like You.*

*Thank You for loving me. I praise You for working in my life and helping me to change.*

*I thank You for wiping my sins away. Thank You for the promise of not rejecting a broken and repentant heart (Psalm 51:17).*

*May Your kingdom come, and Your will be done in the sight of many witnesses.*

*In Your precious, holy name I pray.*
*AMEN.*

# A Prodigal Prayer

Prodigal simply means wayward or lost. As much as we might contest the label, we have all been prodigal at some point in our lives. In the story of the Prodigal Son, we find the beautiful illustration of God's unconditional love for each and every one of us.

In the beginning of the story, we find two sons. The youngest asks his father to give him his inheritance before he dies. The father obliges the request. A few days later, the younger son packs his belongings and sets a course for a distant land where he wastes all of his money on wild living.

When the son's money ran out, a famine had hit the land and he began to starve. Upon persuading a local farmer to hire him, he was sent into the field to feed the farmer's pigs. The son was so hungry that even the pig's food looked good to him, but he wasn't even allowed to eat that!

It is at this point that the prodigal son comes to his senses. He has a broken spirit and a contrite heart. He realizes that he has committed a great wrong by wandering far from home—the place where he was loved and cared for. He acknowledges that he does not even deserve to be called his father's son, but longs to be his father's servant. He longs to return home.

And, when the son returns home, the reception he receives is better than he could possibly imagine. His father kills the fatted calf, gives him a robe, a ring, and an elaborate celebration (Luke 15:11-31).

Do you need to return home today? Deuteronomy 4:30 says, "In the distant future, when you are suffering all these things, you will finally return to the Lord your God and listen to what he tells you."

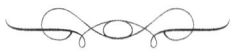

*Dear Heavenly Father,*

*I want to come home to You. I do not even deserve to be called Your son/daughter. Forgive me for wandering so very far away from You. Please accept me back as Your servant, Lord.*

*Thank You for Your goodness and love, Father. I long to dwell with You forever. Help me to never wander away. You are my place of protection and rest.*

*Thank You for rejoicing in me, Father. I rejoice in You! You are my Savior and my King.*

*Thank You for rescuing me. Teach me Your will and Your way. May I safely abide with You now and always.*

*For it is in Your holy name I pray.*
*AMEN.*

# A Prayer for Humility

"True humility and fear of the Lord lead to riches, honor, and long life" (Proverbs 22:4).

Moses was a very humble man. The *Holy Bible* tells us in Numbers 12:3 that he was, "more humble than any other person on earth."

But Moses' brother and sister became proud and began to complain about Moses. Miriam and Aaron criticized Moses for marrying a Cushite woman. They referred to themselves as God's messengers, too, along with Moses. God heard them and punished them for their pride. Miriam was struck white with leprosy. Upon seeing her, Aaron begged for forgiveness.

Moses offered a prayer asking God to heal Miriam. Miriam was kept outside the camp for seven days and was then accepted back. Something tells me that during those seven days, Miriam was cleansed from much more than just her leprosy.

2 Samuel 22:28 says, "You rescue the humble, but your eyes watch the proud and humiliate them."

My mother has said, "We should all enjoy a healthy slice of humble pie on occasion." To which my father responds, "Yes, humility tastes much better than humiliation." I can attest to the truth of both statements.

Are you facing a crisis of humiliation? 2 Chronicles 7:14 says, "Then if my people who are called by my name will humble themselves and pray and seek my face and turn from their wicked ways, I will hear from heaven and will forgive their sins and restore their land."

Jesus tells us in Matthew 5:5, "God blesses those who are humble, for they will inherit the whole earth." And, Matthew 18:4 says, "So anyone who becomes as humble as this little child is the greatest in the Kingdom of Heaven."

*Dear Heavenly Father,*

*Please forgive me for having a haughty heart. Cleanse me of all pride, Lord. I know that I am nothing apart from You. I thank You and praise You for being my source for all things, Father.*

*Forgive me for relying on worldly wisdom that is only foolishness to You (1 Corinthians 3:19).*

*Give me the heart of a child, Father, that I may be pleasing to You. Make me humble, that I may grow in Your wisdom (Proverbs 11:2). Lead me in doing what is right, Lord. Teach me Your ways.*

*I praise You for Your love, Your power, and Your gentle goodness at work in my life, Lord. May I be content to dwell with You forever.*

*In Your precious, holy name I pray.*
*AMEN.*

# A Prayer for Revival

"The Lord heard Elijah's prayer, and the life of the child returned, and he revived" (1 Kings 17:22)!

This is a great story. There was a certain widow living in the village of Zarephath, where God had sent Elijah to live. Elijah found the widow gathering sticks and asked her for a cup of water and some bread. The widow replied that she had no bread and only enough flour and oil for one last meal for herself and her son.

Elijah told the widow not to be afraid, and asked her to do as she had planned, but to make some bread for him first, for God promised that she would have provision until the famine passed. The woman did as Elijah said, and there was food for all of them for many days!

Sometime later, the widow's son became ill and died. The widow was so terribly upset that she picked up her son and took him to Elijah, blaming him for her son's death. Elijah was a humble servant of God. He took the boy to his room upstairs in the widow's home.

1 Kings 17:21-24 tells us what happened next, "And he stretched himself out over the child three times and cried out to the Lord, 'O Lord my God, please let this child's life return to him.' The Lord heard Elijah's prayer, and the life of the child returned, and he revived! Then Elijah brought him down from the upper room and gave him to his mother. 'Look!' he said. 'Your son is alive!'

Then the woman told Elijah, 'Now I know for sure that you are a man of God, and that the Lord truly speaks through you.'"

Sometimes as Christians we live as though we were dead. Let us pray for God to revive our hearts for His glory.

*Dear Heavenly Father,*

*Revive us! We live as though we are dead to You. Help us to be dead to sin, but alive to You, Father!*

*Fill us with Your holy, zealous fire. Rekindle our hearts with Your love, goodness, and unfailing love raining down from Heaven, Lord.*

*Send revival to our hearts and lives, to our families, to our churches, to our neighborhoods, our schools, our cities, our states, our countries, and, Father, to our world! Set us all ablaze with Your holy, loving fire, Lord.*

*Guard us and protect our bodies, hearts, souls, spirits and emotions from any and all evil intentions, Father.*

*Keep us close to You. Fill each and every heart around us with Your love.*

*Hallelujah! We praise You that Yours is the kingdom and the power and the glory forever and ever.*

*AMEN.*

# A Prayer for Families Struggling with Addiction

Addiction is selfishness wrapped in self-destruction. It is the picture of a person who has become so self-absorbed in their pet sins that they no longer think of anything or anyone except themselves and satisfying their own selfish desires. It is narcissism at its peak. It is the absence of reality. It is the absence of God. It is a sickness. It is sin. And, much like Satan, it wears many different masks.

We give it pretty medical titles and clinical terms to sugar-coat it, but it is simply sin. This type of Godlessness is devastating to families. Families struggle to understand and to cope with how their loved ones can be so deeply lost in darkness.

John 3:19 in *The Message* puts it like this, "This is the crisis we're in: God-light streamed into the world, but men and women everywhere ran for the darkness. They went for the darkness because they were not really interested in pleasing God. Everyone who makes a practice of doing evil, addicted to denial and illusion, hates God-light and won't come near it, fearing a painful exposure. But anyone working and living in truth and reality welcomes God-light so the work can be seen for the God-work it is."

We cannot change the sinner. But we can show the sinner God's light at work in our life. We cannot be tolerant of the sin. But we can love the sinner as Christ loved us and gave Himself for us.

And, we can pray.

"Confess your sins to each other and pray for each other so that you may be healed. The earnest prayer of a righteous person has great power and produces wonderful results" (James 5:16).

*Dear Heavenly Father,*

*Forgive me of my many sins. You know them all. Cleanse me from my unrighteousness.*

*Lord, I come before You now with a concern for _____ who is struggling with _____. I pray that he/she would step out of the darkness of this sin and into Your holy, loving light of truth, Father.*

*Help him/her to see this addiction as sin, Father, and to begin to step into reality—able to see Your truth.*

*Father, help us to be an example of all that is true, right and good. Give us the words to say and help us to know what actions to take and when to take them. Grant us Your strength, Lord, because we are struggling.*

*May we all grow deeper in our relationship with You as a result of this struggle, Father.*

*We commit the outcome to You, for it is in Your most holy and precious name we pray.*

*AMEN.*

# A Prayer of Praise

*Dear Lord,*

*I praise You for the black of night*
*For through it I can see Your light*
*I praise You through life's stormy seas*
*For here, You bring me to my knees*
*I praise You in death's gloomy grave*
*Knowing Christ my soul did save*
*I praise you when I'm all alone*
*For here, I see you on Your throne*
*I praise You when I sing my song*
*For You have held me all day long*
*In all these things I give You praise*
*For You are with me all my days.*

# Author Biography

**PRISCILLA DOREMUS** is the daughter of a Baptist Minister who has enjoyed writing from the time she was big enough to hold a pencil. At age ten, she published *The Mysterious Mansion* in *Highlights* with the assistance of her uncle, Alan Cliburn, an established author.

She holds a Bachelor of Business Administration from Baylor University and a Master's in Educational Administration from the University of Houston—Victoria. She has worked for numerous years in the field of Insurance and Risk Management. Priscilla considers herself a homebody though she has traveled all over the world. She also enjoys baking and has become known around town for her chocolate chip cookies.

Diagnosed with a brain tumor in 2001, something Priscilla sees as one of the most wonderful blessings she ever received, she decided to get serious about writing. *Prayers for Times of Crisis* was her first nonfiction work.

Priscilla is a married mother of two grown children. She and her family currently live in Sugar Land, Texas, together with the family dog, Little Bear.

www.ingramcontent.com/pod-product-compliance
Lightning Source LLC
Chambersburg PA
CBHW021059080526
44587CB00010B/309